The Second World War

'The last time there was cheering'

NEIL DEMARCO

Contents

Chapter 1	Appeasement, 1938–39: Was Chamberlain Right?	2
Chapter 2	The War in Europe, 1939–45: An Overview	4
Chapter 3	*Blitzkrieg*	6
Chapter 4	German Advances, 1939–40	8
Chapter 5	The Battle of Britain	12
Chapter 6	Italy, and the War in North Africa	14
Chapter 7	Nazi Occupation and Resistance	16
Chapter 8	Barbarossa: The German Invasion of Russia	18
Chapter 9	German Defeat in Russia	20
Chapter 10	From the Normandy Landings to Berlin	22
Chapter 11	How Effective Was the Bombing of Germany?	24
Chapter 12	The War in the Atlantic	26
Chapter 13	Why Did Germany Lose the War?	28
Chapter 14	Pearl Harbor	30
Chapter 15	The United States Strikes Back	32
Chapter 16	Why Was Japan Defeated?	34
Chapter 17	The Propaganda War	36
Chapter 18	The Blitz	38
Chapter 19	Evacuation	44
Chapter 20	Food Supplies and Rationing	46
Chapter 21	Women in the Workforce	48
Chapter 22	Women in the Armed Forces	50
Chapter 23	'The Friendly Invasion' – GIs and British Women	52
Chapter 24	How Far Did the Role of Women Really Change?	54
Chapter 25	How Did the War Affect the Workers?	56
Chapter 26	How Good Was Churchill as a War Leader?	58
Chapter 27	How Did the War Change Britain?	60
Glossary		64
Index		Inside back cover

Hodder & Stoughton

A MEMBER OF THE HODDER HEADLINE GROUP

Appeasement, 1938–39: Was Chamberlain Right?

Why did Chamberlain support appeasement? What difference did events in Czechoslovakia make? Did appeasement make war more likely?

Appeasement is the term used to describe the foreign policies of the Conservative governments of Stanley Baldwin (1935–37) and Neville Chamberlain (1937–40). Appeasement involved making concessions to the two main **dictators** of Europe, Hitler of Germany and Mussolini of Italy. The hope was that by making concessions to them another terrible war, like the First World War, could be avoided.

Opponents of appeasement have argued that it was a shameful and cowardly policy of giving in to bullies to keep Britain out of a war. Supporters of appeasement have argued that Baldwin and especially Chamberlain were trying to bring about an end to the quarrels in Europe. These quarrels went back to the end of the First World War.

The Treaty of Versailles

The treaty which ended the First World War, the Treaty of Versailles of 1919, left Germany a bitter nation. Italy felt cheated too. Politicians at the time believed that as long as Germany felt this way there would never be lasting peace in Europe. Chamberlain agreed with this opinion and he took a favourable view of Hitler's complaints about how unfair the treaty had been to Germany. He believed that if Germany's complaints were dealt with fairly then Europe could look forward to a long period of peace.

This wasn't Chamberlain's only reason for supporting appeasement. Britain was still suffering from the effects of the Great Depression and Chamberlain was reluctant to spend vast sums of money on improving the country's armed forces. Weak defences, he believed, wouldn't matter if Britain avoided war. Britain was more worried about defending its empire and had been concerned about the threat from Japan in the Far East. It couldn't deal with aggression from both Germany and Japan. Besides, public opinion supported appeasement and Chamberlain, therefore, was only doing what the people wanted.

Many people in Britain believed that much of the Treaty of Versailles was unfair to Germany. Baldwin did little about Hitler sending in troops to the Rhineland in 1936 because of this. Chamberlain agreed that Germany should be able to unite with Austria in 1938. After all, the Austrians were Germans, just as the Rhineland was German. But the situation was different when Hitler claimed the Sudetenland region of Czechoslovakia.

Sept. 1939: Germany invaded Poland

August 1939: Germany and the Soviet Union secretly agreed to invade Poland together

March 1939: Germany seized the rest of Czechoslovakia

Oct. 1938: Germany allowed to occupy the Sudetenland

March 1936: German troops marched into Rhineland, breaking the Treaty of Versailles

March 1938: Austria united with Germany, breaking the Treaty of Versailles

CZECHO-SLOVAKIA

SWITZER-LAND

AUSTRIA

SPAIN

ITALY

A How Germany expanded its borders, 1936–9.

'Czechoslovakia: Now You See It ...'

The Sudetenland contained 70 per cent of Czech industry and included arms factories. Its population was mostly German and there were three million of them. In September 1938 Hitler demanded that Czechoslovakia hand over the Sudetenland and its population to Germany. Czechoslovakia had no intention of giving up the region to Hitler.

Chamberlain saw the Sudetenland in much the same way as he saw Austria. The Sudetenland was basically a German-speaking area and really should belong to Germany. He therefore set out to get the Sudetenland for Hitler – even if this meant ignoring the protests of a democratic

Czechoslovakia. Mussolini arranged a meeting at Munich in Germany on 29 September for Chamberlain, Hitler, himself, and the French Prime Minister, Daladier to discuss the issue.

The four leaders decided that Germany should have all of the Sudetenland straight away. The Czechs, not surprisingly, protested at the decision to give away part of their country without even consulting them! Chamberlain told the Czech leader that they could fight Germany to keep the Sudetenland – but they would have to fight on their own. The Czechs had no choice but to give in.

'... Now You Don't'

A delighted Hitler promised that Germany would demand no more land in Europe. Germany, he declared, was complete. Chamberlain was welcomed back to Britain as a hero for ending the crisis without a war.

Churchill bitterly attacked the Munich Agreement in the House of Commons. In October 1938 he said that Britain had behaved shamefully by giving in to Hitler and abandoning the Czechs. He also argued that Germany's military

> The historian, William Shirer, has written that Britain and France would have easily defeated Germany in October 1938.

power would grow stronger while Britain's armed forces remained weak. If Germany did go to war with Britain or France later, then they would regret the loss of 'the fine Czech army'. The Czech army was well equipped and numbered about 500 000 men – not much smaller than Germany's. Six months later, in March 1939, Hitler ordered German troops to seize the rest of Czechoslovakia. He broke every promise made at Munich.

At last, Chamberlain and Daladier realised that they could not trust Hitler to keep his promises. They both offered Poland an alliance. If Germany invaded Poland, where about a million Germans lived, Britain and France promised to defend the Poles. Hitler took little notice of this alliance. Why should he? Britain and France had done nothing over the Rhineland, the takeover of Austria, the Sudetenland, or even Czechoslovakia. Why should things be any different over Poland?

The Nazi-Soviet Pact

The only country Hitler was worried about was the Soviet Union. He was afraid that a German invasion of Poland might lead to war with the Soviet Union. He did want a war with the world's only **communist** power – but not yet. In late

August 1939 the **Nazis** and the Soviets met and agreed a pact. This was called a non-aggression pact because they promised not to go to war with each other. But secretly they also agreed to invade and divide Poland between them. Germany would invade on 1 September and Russia later in the month.

B 30 September 1938. Chamberlain has just returned from the Munich Conference with 'Herr Hitler'. He has in his right hand the terms of the agreement which promised, Chamberlain claimed, 'peace in our time'. Peace did not last long. It isn't difficult to poke fun at Chamberlain for placing so much trust in the promises of a man like Hitler but it's easy to be clever *after* the events have taken place. Very few people in Britain at the time argued against his policy.

C Aircraft built by Britain, France and Germany, 1937–9:

	1937	1938	1939
France	743	1382	3163
Britain	2153	2827	7940
Germany	5606	5235	8295

1 What was appeasement?
2 What was Chamberlain's basic reason for supporting appeasement?
3 Did Hitler's demands for the Sudetenland fit in with Chamberlain's policy of fair treatment for Germany? Explain your answer.
4 Did Hitler's action in March 1939 fit in with Chamberlain's policy? Explain your answer.
5 'Chamberlain's policy towards Germany was the best that Britain could do in the circumstances.' Using the information in this chapter, explain whether you agree or disagree with this interpretation.

The War in Europe, 1939–45: An Overview

What were the main strategic events of the war? What events marked the turning point between the early victories for the Axis powers and their eventual defeat?

The Second World War in Europe can be roughly divided into two periods. The years between 1939 and early 1942 were mostly years of victory for the **Axis** powers of Germany, Italy and Japan. Towards the end of 1942 the war began to turn against the Axis. From then on, the years between late 1942 and 1945 were ones of triumph for the Allied powers of the USA, the Soviet Union and Britain.

This chapter is a brief outline of the main events of these years.

1939 – early 1942: years of Axis victory

Germany's new form of warfare, *Blitzkrieg*, or lightning war, brought a string of rapid victories. German troops invaded Poland in September 1939 and overran the Polish forces within a month. This was a task made easier by the invasion of eastern Poland by the Soviet Union (Russia) in the same month. The Russians occupied eastern Poland

A After helping to defeat Poland, the Russians attacked Finland in November 1939. The Finnish–Soviet War (November 1939 – March 1940) was not part of the Second World War but it was a very costly victory for the much bigger Soviet forces against the well-equipped Finnish troops (above). The Russian army did so badly that Hitler was convinced – mistakenly – that a German invasion of Russia would be easy.

B RAF cadets training in 1942. At first glance it would seem that these cadets would have to pedal very hard to get airborne and their chances against a German fighter were not very encouraging. In fact, they're practising formation flying.

while the Germans took the western half. This had been agreed in the Nazi-Soviet Pact in August.

The Germans occupied Norway in April 1940. This made sure vital iron ore supplies would continue to reach German factories. It was now that Hitler decided on his boldest move: the invasion of France in May 1940. The conquest of France in June represented the greatest success of Hitler's *Blitzkrieg* strategy.

British forces were driven out of France after their evacuation from the beaches of Dunkirk in June 1940, leaving much valuable equipment behind. But 330 000 British and French troops had escaped. Britain waited for the expected German invasion. The German air force tried to destroy Britain's Royal Air Force during the Battle of Britain in August and September 1940, but failed.

Invasion of Russia

Hitler decided to put aside his plans for the invasion of Britain. His attention was really elsewhere since his main ambition was to conquer Soviet Russia. In June 1941 the decisive event of the war in Europe took place as three million German troops invaded Russia. By 15 October the Germans were only 100 kilometres from Moscow.

The war became a truly world war in December 1941 when Japan launched a surprise attack on the American fleet in its Pacific base at Pearl Harbor and followed this with attacks on British bases in the Far East. Germany and Italy, in support of their Axis partner Japan, declared war on the USA as well. The Japanese captured the British naval base at Singapore in February 1942. They took prisoner 62 000 British, Australian and Indian troops.

Late 1942 – 1945: years of Allied triumph

Italy's declaration of war on Britain and France meant that the war now included North Africa. Here, British forces scored some early successes against the Italians. German troops were sent to the aid of their Axis partner in February 1941. The German–Italian army drove the British back from their earlier conquests. But the Axis run of victories came to an end at the battle of El Alamein in November 1942. Italy itself was invaded in July 1943 and surrendered in September to the Anglo-American forces.

In the same month as El Alamein, the Germans were facing an even more devastating defeat in Russia at Stalingrad. At first, the victories had come easily as the Russian Red Army broke and retreated. At Stalingrad, though, the Russians held their position and turned the tide against Hitler, eventually defeating the Germans in January 1943. The Germans tried one final offensive at the battle of Kursk in July 1943. It failed and from then on the Germans were constantly on the retreat.

The battle of Kursk in July 1943 was the biggest tank battle in history.

The tide turns in the Pacific

Retreat became a new experience for the Japanese as well. After Pearl Harbor Japanese naval and land forces had swept aside all opposition in the Pacific. But the naval battle of Midway in June 1942 put a stop to these victories as the Americans sank four Japanese aircraft carriers. 1944 saw two further decisive American victories at sea over the Japanese: the battles of the Philippine Sea (June) and Leyte Gulf (October).

Germany's failure against Russia convinced the British and Americans that the time was right to strike a blow against German-occupied Europe in the west. In June 1944 Allied forces landed on the beaches of Normandy in France. The surprised Germans were unable to drive the Allies back into the sea and in August Paris was freed from Nazi rule.

The Allies made slow progress from the west while the Russians advanced from the east. There was a setback for the British at Arnhem in September 1944. The Germans made one final – and unsuccessful – effort to prevent an invasion of Germany itself. In December they launched the Ardennes Offensive (or 'the Battle of the Bulge'). Early in 1945 Allied troops moved into German territory and the Russians occupied Berlin in April. Hitler shot himself at the end of that month and on 8 May 1945 Germany surrendered. The war in Europe was over.

In April 1945 the Americans took Okinawa and from there they could launch an invasion of Japan itself. In August the USA decided to make use of their new, secret weapon. Two atomic bombs were dropped: one each on the cities of Hiroshima and Nagasaki. A week later on 15 August the Emperor of Japan, Hirohito, agreed to surrender. The formal surrender was signed in September 1945. The Second World War was over.

Q

Read through this chapter and then copy and complete the chart below so that it shows each important event in the war. The dates up to 1943 have already been listed. Complete the second and third columns for each date.

Date	Description	Victory for
1939 September	Germany invaded Poland	Germany
September		
1940 April		
May		
June		
June		
August – September		
1941 June		
December		
December	Germany and Italy declared war on the United States	
1942 February		
June		
November – January 1943		

Blitzkrieg

What was *Blitzkrieg*? Why was it so effective?

Hitler had prepared for a short but vigorous war. Germany had a *small* number of well-trained and equipped mechanised units: tanks, supported by motorised infantry (troops in trucks). It was vital for Hitler that the war he planned was both short and limited. This was because Germany didn't have enough supplies or weapons to fight a long war on more than one front.

Artillery and dive bombers began the process by 'softening up' the enemy. They shelled the enemy front and rear, increasing panic and fear. The panic created among the civilian population had two purposes. It damaged morale and also drove thousands of frightened civilians onto the roads. These civilians jammed the roads as they fled away from the fighting. At the same time, the troops of the country being attacked were trying to use the same roads to bring up reserves. Confusion took over.

A French troops are shown here digging trenches 'somewhere behind the Maginot Line'. This sums up France's problem in 1940. They were expecting the wrong war, at the wrong place in the wrong way.

Surprise is the key

Surprise was a key factor in the German success. The attacks on Poland and Soviet Russia were surprise ones. Most of the Polish air force, like the Russian one later in 1941, was so unprepared that it was destroyed on the ground. The French had less excuse because they had been at war with Germany for nine months when they were attacked. What surprised them, though, was the direction of the attack (see Chapter 4). Once again, Hitler had seized the decisive initiative.

Germany's *Blitzkrieg* strategy concentrated armoured columns of tanks and troops in lorries at the key, weak points of the enemy defences. They used their concentrated fire-power, speed, and greater numbers at these points to smash their way through the enemy's positions. They went round the better-defended positions and cut them off from reinforcements. The infantry on foot could deal with these later. While this was happening paratroops were busy seizing enemy HQs, telephone exchanges, or bridges. Then they would wait for their own fast-moving armoured columns to catch up with them.

Why was the German strategy so successful?

Clearly surprise, speed and concentrated fire-power were very important but these cannot explain everything. The Poles, the French, the British, and later the Russians, all confronted the Germans with outdated tactics. They had failed to understand the vital role that the tank would play in the war. The tank should be an independent weapon and not tied down by having to protect slow-moving infantry.

German equipment was not really any better than that of the Allies. Indeed, the best tank of the war at this stage was French, and the best tank of the whole war was the Russian T34. Germany's armed forces weren't any bigger but they were put to better use. Both the British and French used their tanks in small numbers, spread thinly among their troops. The Germans *grouped* their tanks in highly effective armoured units. In this way, the German tanks were always able to outnumber those of their enemy because the Germans chose where they would fight their battles.

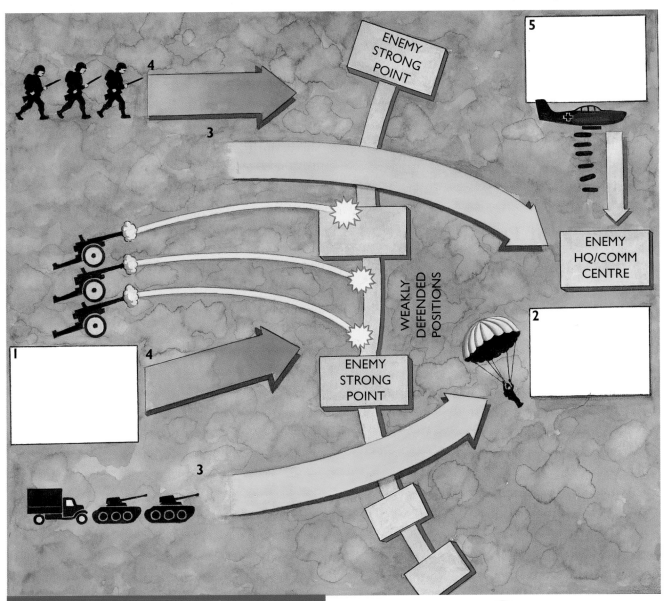

B A typical German *Blitzkrieg* attack.

The idea that the Germans had huge amounts of advanced, new equipment, and that this explains the success of *Blitzkrieg* isn't really true. It is true that when the Germans invaded Russia in 1941 they had 3600 tanks (the Russians had between 10 000 and 15 000) but they also used 650 000 horses. The British and French had more tanks than the Germans in 1940. But the Germans did have a crucial advantage in aircraft numbers. This was important in helping them achieve their stunning victory in 1940. But it wasn't the most important reason, as the next chapter will show. These statistics suggest that Germany's early success was due more to good planning and strategy than having more and better weapons.

The ideas behind *Blitzkrieg* were first put forward by a British officer, Major-General Fuller.

Q

1 Why was it important for Germany to fight only a short and limited war?
2 Why was it important for the success of *Blitzkrieg* to cause panic among the enemy civilians?
3 Look at source B. Copy the illustration into your file and then fill in the blank spaces on the illustration using the correct labels from the following:
(A) Parachutists dropped behind enemy lines to capture key positions such as bridges and HQs until relieved by armoured columns coming up in support. (B) Infantry on foot follow up to deal with enemy strong points. (C) Tanks and troops in lorries bypass enemy strong points. (D) Artillery shell enemy front lines and rear positions. (E) Dive bombers attack enemy troop reinforcements.

German Advances, 1939–40

Why were there several defeats for the Allies after the 'phoney war'? Was the evacuation at Dunkirk a miracle or a disaster?

The defeat of Poland

Hitler had a plan for the political domination of Europe. He intended to create a German empire in which the east European states would provide *Lebensraum* (living space) for his German master race. This meant, to begin with, the conquest of Poland and then the Soviet Union (though the Russians, of course, didn't know this). The Germans occupied Poland without too much difficulty by the end of September, after launching their surprise invasion on 1 September. Poland's problems were made that much worse when the Russians invaded from the east on 17 September. This had been agreed between Russia and Germany in their non-aggression pact in August.

Britain and France both had a treaty with Poland and declared war on Germany on 3 September. But this made little difference to Poland. The British and French chose not to do the one thing they could have done to save Poland. This was to invade Germany while the bulk of the German armed forces were involved in Poland. The British and French (not to mention the Poles) were to pay a heavy price for this reluctance to begin the war seriously.

For the British and French the first seven months of the war were rather dull – there was no fighting on land between them and the Germans. This period (September 1939 – April 1940) was called at the time the 'phoney war'. Instead of making jokes about the 'Bore war' or 'Sitzkrieg' (because there wasn't much fighting during these months), the British and French should have been learning the lessons of *Blitzkrieg*. Unfortunately, the Allied High Commands decided that Germany's crushing victory over the Poles was due to the poor quality of the Polish armed forces and not to the German strategy.

Invasion of Norway

The phoney war came to a dramatic end in April 1940 when Germany invaded and occupied Norway. Norway was important to Germany for three reasons. First, Germany's supply of iron ore

from Sweden came through the Norwegian port of Narvik during the winter. In 1939 Sweden provided nearly 30 per cent of Germany's iron ore. Secondly, Norway's west coast would provide useful air and naval bases for attacks on Britain. Later, once Russia was in the war, Norway offered good bases for attacks on Allied convoys to Russia. The British and French troops sent to oppose the Germans achieved little.

A Germany's *Blitzkrieg* depended on surprise and speed of movement for its success. The enemy would be attacked at its weakest points with overwhelming force.

The loss of Norway was a setback which led to a new government in Britain. Chamberlain, Britain's Prime Minister since 1937, was widely seen as the man who had failed to stop Hitler and Parliament decided a more aggressive leader was needed. That man was Winston Churchill. He had long been a critic of Chamberlain's appeasement policy before the war and didn't think much of Chamberlain's half-hearted efforts against Germany during it. He became Prime Minister of a **coalition government** of Conservatives, Labour and Liberals on 10 May.

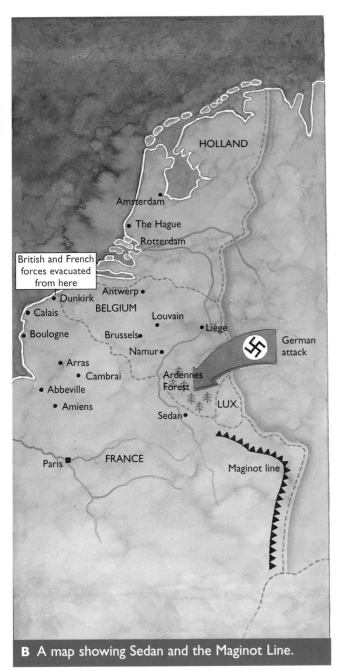

HOLLAND

Amsterdam

The Hague

Rotterdam

British and French forces evacuated from here

Dunkirk

Antwerp

BELGIUM

Calais

Louvain

Boulogne

Brussels

Liège

Namur

Arras

Cambrai

Ardennes Forest

Abbeville

LUX.

Amiens

Sedan

Paris

FRANCE

Maginot line

German attack

B A map showing Sedan and the Maginot Line.

The French High Command was sure that their expensive line of underground forts,

German tanks in France in 1940 filled up at petrol stations as they attacked.

the Maginot Line, would protect France from a German attack. It probably would have done – if the Germans had decided to attack the Line, but they didn't. A key feature of *Blitzkrieg* was that the attackers *avoided* the enemy's strong points. The Maginot Line only protected France along its border with Germany. Hitler decided to attack at Sedan on France's border with Belgium.

'I hope the Tommies are good swimmers'

The Germans broke through at Sedan to the astonishment of the French. The French had thought that the Ardennes Forest, to the north east of Sedan, was too dense for tanks to pass through. French resistance crumbled as the German tanks raced to the Channel coast in an effort to cut off the retreat of the 250 000 strong British Expeditionary Force. Guderian, the German tank commander, covered a remarkable 320 kilometres in ten days. But for once, caution got the better of Hitler and he ordered Guderian to halt his advance on Dunkirk. This was the port from which the BEF and some of the French army would try to escape to Britain.

The British and French at Dunkirk would have been destroyed if Guderian had been allowed to attack with his 200 or so tanks. But Hitler, it seems, was confident of an easy victory. He wanted to save his tanks for the attack on Paris. Goering, the commander of the Luftwaffe (German air force), convinced Hitler that the Luftwaffe could easily finish off the Allied forces at Dunkirk and destroy their rescue vessels. 'I hope the Tommies [the British] are good swimmers' he boasted to Hitler.

The fall of France

The loss of Norway was a setback to the Allies, but worse was to follow in May. On 10 May Germany invaded Belgium, Holland and then France. Once again, the Germans caught their enemies unprepared. The overwhelming defeat of France in just six weeks was Hitler's greatest military campaign of the war. He planned and carried it out against the advice of his more cautious generals. But, as on other occasions, the victory was mostly due to the fine quality of his troops and the bungled plans and efforts of his enemies.

Q

1 What lesson had the Allied High Commands failed to learn from the defeat of Poland?
2 Why was Norway so useful to the Germans?
3 a) Why was Sedan a good place for the German attack in 1940?
   b) Why, nonetheless, were the French taken by surprise?
4 Why were the British and French troops lucky to escape from Dunkirk?

DUNKIRK – THE MAKING OF A MYTH?

The British government had hoped that as many as 50 000 troops would be rescued from France. In the event, over 225 000 British and 110 000 French troops managed to escape from Dunkirk by ship between 26 May and 3 June 1940. This happened mostly by night when the Luftwaffe could not operate. It was a remarkable achievement right under the noses of the encircling Germans. The British press and radio hailed the evacuation – Operation Dynamo – as the 'miracle of Dunkirk'.

A number of factors contributed to this achievement. Many of the German bombs failed to explode when they hit the soft sand. RAF fighters fought off many of the German aircraft. Most of the 850 ships involved were owned by civilians. They sailed across the Channel and ferried men from the beaches to the bigger Royal Navy vessels. Sometimes they even sailed all the way back to the English coast. 250 of the rescue ships were sunk. However, the British did have the satisfaction of knowing that their wrecks now clogged up the harbour at Dunkirk and made it useless to the Germans.

France betrayed?

But it was also a shattering defeat. Britain had clearly abandoned its only ally as well as huge amounts of vital equipment – 475 tanks and 1000 artillery guns were left behind. The French felt betrayed. In the early stages of the evacuation only one French soldier was being taken off the beaches of Dunkirk for every ten British soldiers. The French complained and Churchill issued

B Newspapers, like the *Daily Mail* quoted here, covered the evacuation of Dunkirk in glowing, heroic terms. This extract is from one reporter's interviews with the men evacuated back to England on 1 June 1940.

An artillery man told me that with thousands of others he had spent two days among the sand dunes with little food and no shelter from the German dive bombers.

Yet the men still joked, played cards and even started a football game to keep up their spirits … A sailor told me that a vessel in which he had been assisting on the Belgian coast had been sunk. No sooner had he and all his comrades landed [in England] than they all volunteered to go back at once.

A Norman Wilkinson, an official war artist at the time, painted *Little Ships at Dunkirk*. A variety of vessels can be seen: a Royal Navy destroyer with a German bomb exploding nearby; Thames sailing barges; a large yacht still painted in peacetime white; coasters towing lifeboats packed with soldiers.

orders that French troops should be treated the same as the British. The evacuation had only been possible because 40 000 French troops defended Dunkirk from the encircling Germans. Most of these were later captured by the Germans.

C The official view of Dunkirk was of a heroic event with 225 000 disciplined and gallant British troops just waiting to hit back at the 'beastly Nazis'. This was accepted until the late 1950s and early 1960s. Then historians began to question it. Did it really happen like that? Phillip Knightley wrote this in 1975 (in *The First Casualty*), commenting on the research carried out by another historian, Richard Collier:

Collier quoted accounts of a hotel cellar in Dunkirk packed with British and French troops singing, weeping and screaming drunk; of groups of men, deserted by their officers. A corporal kept order in his boat, filled with troops crazy with fear, by threatening to shoot the first one who disobeyed him. As for the survivors arriving in Britain itching to return for another crack at the enemy, this may have been true of the army as a whole, but Collier found a Kentish police inspector … who remembered only too well the sight of discouraged men hurling their rifles from the trains carrying them from Dover.

The French felt even more angry when Churchill refused to send 120 Spitfires to France to help the French air force.

Churchill took a realistic view of Dunkirk. 'Wars are not won by evacuations,' he told the House of Commons.

As far as Churchill was concerned, these planes were now needed to defend Britain as France was clearly beaten.

France surrendered on 22 June and the Germans got hold of two years' worth of oil supplies. Hitler allowed a pro-German French government, led by Marshall Petain, to rule the south of France from the town of Vichy. This area became known as **Vichy France**. The north of France and its west coast were directly under the control of the Germans. A similar development took place in Norway where a Norwegian Nazi, **Quisling**, headed the pro-German government there.

D British troops returning from Dunkirk, 2 June 1940, full of cheery 'Dunkirk spirit'. The original caption for this photograph commented approvingly on how this British soldier had come back with a captured German rifle. This may have come in handy. Later, censored reports told of British troops throwing their rifles out of carriage windows so quite a few soldiers must have had no rifle at all.

Q

1 Why could the British celebrate the evacuation at Dunkirk as a miracle?
2 Why was the French view less enthusiastic?
3 Why would the British government in 1940 have approved of:
   a) the painting in source A
   b) the article in the Daily Mail in source B?
4 The interpretation of the events concerning Dunkirk in source C is very different from the views in sources A and B. What reasons can you give to explain this difference in interpretation? (Remember to think about the **provenance** of each source – especially when they were painted or written.)

Extended writing
'Germany's Blitzkrieg was successful more because of the Allies weaknesses than because of Germany's strengths.' Write an essay of about 300 words explaining whether you agree or disagree with this statement. The following points will help you:
● the quality of military equipment on each side;
● the differences between each side over military tactics;
● Britain's approach to war before Churchill became Prime Minister;
● France's faith in the Maginot Line.

The Battle of Britain

Why did Hitler postpone his plan to invade Britain?

After the fall of France, Britain expected a German invasion at any time. But before it could take place the Germans had to gain control of the skies. To do this they had to destroy the Royal Air Force (RAF). The Battle of Britain from July to September 1940 was fought between the RAF and the Luftwaffe to see who would control those skies. This battle would decide whether an invasion would take place or not. German troops could only be transported across the Channel if they were safe from attack by the RAF.

After France's defeat Hitler had offered peace terms to Britain. Some members of the British government, such as Lord Halifax and Neville Chamberlain, were keen to discuss these terms. They believed that Britain had little chance of resisting a German invasion but Churchill was not interested in negotiating with Hitler. Britain would fight on and his stubborn defiance helped to inspire the British through the next six, dark months. In the meantime, all that stood between Britain and a German invasion were 800 RAF fighter planes, under the command of Air Chief Marshall Dowding.

7 September 1940

To begin with, Goering, the Luftwaffe commander, followed a sensible strategy. He bombed radar stations, fighter bases and, in early September, aircraft factories. By the middle of August the Germans were convinced that the RAF had only 300 fighters left. In fact, the number was 600. Goering, therefore, concentrated on a target he knew that Dowding would have to defend: fighter airfields. By doing this, he was sure he could destroy the RAF's few remaining fighter planes.

The RAF was finding it very difficult to make up its losses in pilots and the battle was going in Germany's favour – but the Germans didn't know it. The victory over the RAF which Goering had promised in August seemed no nearer in September. Hitler lost patience.

> Spitfire pilots' greatest fear was death by burning. The petrol tank was just in front of their seats.

A Fighter pilots 'scrambling' for their Spitfires. The Spitfire was the best fighter plane of the war in 1940 but Hurricanes played a bigger role in the RAF's victory. The pilots shown here are 'Free French' – those who chose to continue fighting alongside Britain under the command of de Gaulle rather than surrender to the Germans in June 1940.

B German night-time bombing led to a black-out of city streets. The white line seen here on the pavement was to keep pedestrians from walking into each other by keeping on one side of the line. The black-out also applied to cars' headlights at first. But, after 1500 people had been killed in road accidents by December 1939, the government allowed cars to be driven with headlamp covers with small slits in them.

7 September proved to be a turning point. On this day Hitler, outraged by a British bombing raid on Berlin, ordered a switch in tactics. He told Goering to bomb London and other major cities in an effort to terrorise Britain into surrender. For Dowding, this brought welcome relief. The factories could turn out 500 fighters a week and the damaged airfields could be repaired as the Luftwaffe concentrated on less vital targets like London.

Sea Lion postponed

The bombing of Britain's cities, the Blitz, continued until May 1941 but Hitler had already given up on 'Operation Sea Lion' – the plan for the invasion of Britain – as early as mid-October 1940.

Hitler's real ambitions were to the east. His chief concern was to invade Russia. He decided to leave Britain alone for the time being since, in his view, Britain was no threat to Germany anyway.

The RAF was able to defeat the Germans mostly because of the foolish change in tactics on 7 September. The Spitfire – the best fighter plane at the time – also helped, as did radar. Radar gave advance warning of air attacks and allowed the enemy to be intercepted long before it reached its target. In this way Dowding was able to concentrate his limited number of fighter planes at the right point at the right time. It's worth adding, also, that Hitler was probably never really that interested in invading Britain.

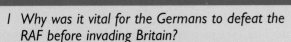

1 Why was it vital for the Germans to defeat the RAF before invading Britain?

2 Why were fighter airfields, radar station and aircraft factories sensible targets for the Germans to bomb?

3 Why was 7 September such a key turning point in the battle?

4 How close do you think Britain was to defeat in 1940? In your answer, think about: the condition the RAF was in; the switch in German tactics on 7 September; Hitler's other plans.

5 Why were the Germans so successful in the early stages of the war? The table below contains five reasons which help to explain the early successes of the German armed forces. These reasons, as they stand, are only general statements. Your task is to copy the chart into your file and then review the chapters so far to find evidence from the text which supports these statements. Copy this into the second column. In the third column you should write a comment of your own, assessing the importance of each of these reasons. One example has already been done for you.

Reason	Evidence	Importance
1 Germany's armed forces were better prepared and trained for their new Blitzkrieg style of warfare.	The Germans grouped their tanks together and concentrated their attacks at the weak points of the enemy defences.	The Allies were taken by surprise by this tactic and lost several key campaigns in Poland, Norway and France.
2 Germany acquired vital supplies of raw materials from the countries it conquered.		
3 There were groups in the occupied countries who were willing to collaborate (co-operate) with the Germans.		
4 The British and French were not ready for the new style of warfare and used out-of-date tactics.		
5 Germany chose the place and moment for attack and so always had surprise on its side.		

Italy, and the War in North Africa

Why were Mussolini's dreams of a new Roman Empire under fascism totally defeated? Why did the Italian Campaign not provide the expected quick victories for the Allies?

The defeat of Italy, September 1943

Mussolini, the fascist dictator of Italy, declared war on France and Britain on 10 June 1940. He was sure at that time that France was beaten (which it was) and that Britain would soon follow (which it did not). The war proved a disaster for Italy and Mussolini. Mussolini was eventually overthrown in July 1943 by a vote of his own fascist party. The King of Italy, Victor Emmanuel, then ordered his arrest.

Fascism, fairly popular when Italy was at peace, was quickly abandoned by the Italians after a series of humiliating failures against the British in North Africa. Italy surrendered to the British and Americans in September 1943, then changed sides and declared war on Germany in October of that year.

The war in North Africa

Mussolini had been desperate to recreate the glories of the Ancient Roman Empire for Italy. This meant carving out a new Italian Empire in the Mediterranean and North Africa by seizing British colonies in Africa.

For this reason he invaded British-controlled Egypt

Mussolini told Italians that it was better to live one day as a lion than a hundred years as a sheep.

from the Italian colony of Libya in September 1940. The Italian troops' equipment was greatly inferior to that of the British. None of the Italian anti-tank guns, for example, could stop a British tank. The troops were poorly led and their morale was low. After some initial success, the large Italian army was driven back and soon was in rapid retreat. This led the Germans in February 1941 to enter the war in North Africa to support Italy with a small force of some four divisions (about 60 000 men).

El Alamein

The Italian–German army was able to turn the tables on the British and in just four months

A Mussolini reviewing the 220 000 troops of the Italian Eighth Army. These were Italy's best equipped and trained troops. Mussolini should have used them in North Africa where they were desperately needed. Instead they were sent to Russia and perished at Stalingrad.

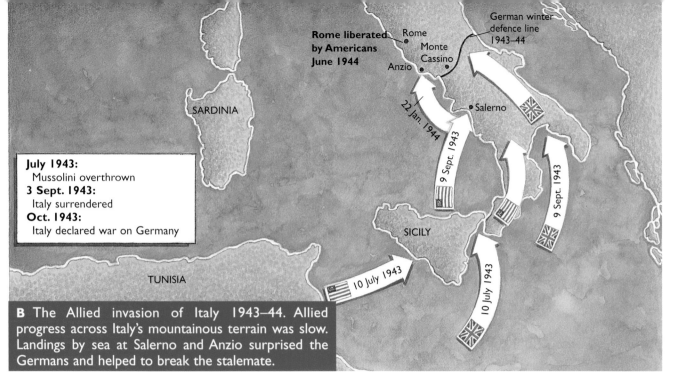

On the map:

Rome liberated by Americans June 1944

Rome

German winter defence line 1943–44

Monte Cassino

Anzio

22 Jan. 1944

Salerno

9 Sept. 1943

SARDINIA

9 Sept. 1943

SICILY

10 July 1943

10 July 1943

TUNISIA

July 1943:
Mussolini overthrown
3 Sept. 1943:
Italy surrendered
Oct. 1943:
Italy declared war on Germany

B The Allied invasion of Italy 1943–44. Allied progress across Italy's mountainous terrain was slow. Landings by sea at Salerno and Anzio surprised the Germans and helped to break the stalemate.

recovered the ground which the Italians had lost earlier. Indeed, the German commander, Rommel, threatened to capture the Suez Canal – a vital link with Britain's empire in the east. However, Rommel's string of victories came to an end at the battle of El Alamein in November 1942. Here Montgomery and the British Eighth Army severely defeated Rommel's German and Italian forces. Montgomery waited patiently until the British forces outnumbered the **Afrika Korps** forces by two to one in men and tanks. The 12-day battle inflicted heavy losses on the Axis. Rommel lost nearly all his 500 tanks, and 60 per cent of his troops were killed, wounded or captured. It was Britain's first real victory over the Germans on land and was a great boost to morale. The Suez Canal and the crucial oil fields beyond it were safe from capture. 100 000 US troops also landed in western North Africa in November, and Rommel's defeat helped to persuade Vichy French forces in the area to surrender to them.

Six months later, what was left of the Italian-German army surrendered in Tunisia. The war in North Africa was over, and Hitler had lost an opportunity to find the oil his forces so desperately needed.

The Italian Campaign, 1943–45

The Anglo-American forces landed in Sicily in July 1943 and then crossed over onto the Italian mainland. As expected Italy quickly surrendered, but the Germans poured over 400 000 troops into the south of the country to hold up the Allied advance. The Germans chose the best defensive positions, such as Monte Cassino, making the most of the mountainous terrain.

The US forces had to bypass Monte Cassino by carrying out a landing by sea some 90 kilometres south of Rome at Anzio in January 1944. Astonishingly, the road to Rome was open as the Germans were taken totally by surprise. However, the very cautious American commander, General Lucas, waited for reinforcements and the Germans quickly blocked the road to Rome. The capital of Italy wasn't captured until June, after more heavy fighting.

Slowly the Allied forces fought their way up the country. Churchill had expected a quick campaign but the Germans were not defeated in Italy until the very end of the war in April 1945. Historians doubt the value of the Italian Campaign in causing Germany's defeat. The Allies lost 300 000 casualties between July 1943 and April 1945. The Germans, it is true, lost more, but these losses didn't seriously weaken their ability to resist the Allied invasion of France in June 1944.

Q

1 Why did Mussolini think June 1940 was a good time to declare war on France and Britain?
2 Why were German troops sent to North Africa in early 1941?
3 Why was El Alamein such an important victory for Britain?
4 Was the Italian Campaign, from the Allies' point of view, worth fighting? Explain your answer.

Nazi Occupation and Resistance

Key Issues **What did the Nazis' racial theory mean for the occupied peoples? How effective were the resistance movements in the occupied countries?**

Nazi racial theory

How the Germans treated occupied peoples depended on their race. Nazi racial theory considered the Danes, Dutch and Norwegians to be of Germanic stock, and Nazi treatment of these people was, at first, mild. The Germans hoped that they would support Germany in its efforts to build a greater German *Reich* or state in Europe.

Some Dutch, Norwegians, and Danes found Nazi promises of an equal role in the new German-dominated Europe attractive. As a result, these Nazi sympathisers, such as Quisling in Norway, collaborated or worked with the Germans. In fact there were collaborators in all areas occupied by the Germans. In France, some helped the Germans round up Jews or gave the names of resistance members to the **Gestapo**, the Nazi secret police.

B The Germans were desperate for workers from the occupied countries to work in their factories in Germany. At first they asked for volunteers, then they used force. 600 000 Frenchmen were sent to work in Germany. This poster tells them that 'When you work in Germany, you will represent French workmanship'.

A These French women, stripped to their underwear, are being paraded through the streets by members of the Resistance. Their crime was to have had sexual relations with German troops – a form of collaboration with the enemy. Such women, though humiliated, usually escaped with their lives. After the war, the Resistance *officially* executed 11 000 collaborators.

The Germans treated harshly from the start those occupied peoples who didn't fit into the Germanic racial category. Poles, Ukrainians and Russians fitted into an 'inferior' racial group called Slavs.

They would be used as slave labour for the Nazi war effort. They would be kept alive only as long as they were useful.

Resistance

Few of the occupied peoples welcomed German occupation. But only a minority were prepared to do anything to oppose or resist their German occupiers. Opposition took two forms: passive and active resistance. Passive resisters didn't use violence but instead might support strikes, demonstrations or hide people hunted by the Gestapo. Danish resisters managed to save 7500 of Denmark's 8000 Jews from arrest and death.

Strikes by railway workers could be especially damaging to the German war effort. In September 1944 Dutch railway workers went on strike to help with the Allied attack at Arnhem. The attack failed and the Dutch were punished severely. The Germans refused food supplies during a famine to the starving population of western Holland. 16 000 died of hunger.

The SOE

Active resisters, though, did use violence against the Germans. Sabotage was a major part of Resistance activity. This involved blowing up railway lines and locomotives, wrecking key machinery in factories, and even attacks on German troops. The British Special Operations Executive (SOE) trained men and women in Britain to help set up resistance groups in occupied Europe. The SOE also provided weapons, radios and explosives. Trained agents were then dropped by parachute into France or wherever they were needed.

C Death by public hanging was one method the Nazis used to discourage resistance activities. This photograph was taken in Belgrade, Yugoslavia.

Reprisals

The acts of sabotage by the French Resistance in Normandy in 1944 led to the destruction of the town of Oradour by the Germans and the massacre of 642 of its population. In June 1942 some British-trained agents parachuted into Czechoslovakia. Against the wishes of the local Resistance, they assassinated the **SS** commander of the region. The Nazi response was the destruction of the town of Lidice and the shooting of 198 men. The women were sent to a **concentration camp** and 98 of their children were kidnapped. The Germanic-looking children were then given to German families.

The dilemma of all Resistance groups was this: should they continue with their activities when they knew that innocent civilians would be shot as **reprisals**? In March 1944 an Italian **partisan** bomb killed 33 German SS troops in Rome. The Germans shot 335 civilians as a reprisal. After the war, some of the relatives of the executed Italians tried unsuccessfully to have the Resistance members put on trial for the deaths of their relatives. In 1997 an 83-year-old former SS captain was sentenced to five years in prison for his role in the massacre.

The Resistance, despite this warning, continued with their attacks. The Germans answered with more massacres (see source D). In October 1944 they shot 1600 men, women and children from a town in central Italy, called Marzabotto.

The activities of Resistance groups were not decisive in the war but they played a valuable role, nonetheless. Sabotage actions by the French Resistance, such as cutting telephone wires, blowing up bridges and railway lines, held up German reinforcements during the D-Day landings. Activities like these meant that the Germans had to keep large numbers of troops in occupied areas. These troops otherwise could have been used in combat against the Allies. But the price paid by local populations for such acts of sabotage was a terrible one.

D The Germans declared that their policy would be to execute 10 hostages for every German killed.

1 Captured partisans are not prisoners of war, and will be shot on the spot.
2 Civilians will also be shot who:
a) supply partisans with (i) food, (ii) shelter, (iii) military information [spying];
b) carry arms (including hunting weapons);
c) commit hostile acts against the German armed forces (particularly tyre and communication wire sabotage).
3 Where partisan bands operate in large numbers, hostages are to be taken first from the population of the district in which they appear. In the case of brutal attacks these men will be shot … If German soldiers fall victim to attacks by civilians, up to ten Italians will be shot for each German killed.

1 Why did the Germans treat peoples like the Danes and Dutch mildly at first?
2 Why do you think some people were prepared to collaborate with the Germans?
3 How useful do you think the activities of Resistance groups were?
4 Do you think people guilty of war crimes committed over 50 years ago should still be put on trial? Explain your answer.
5 If you had been one of the Italian partisans who killed the 33 SS soldiers, would you have owned up to try and save the lives of the hostages? Explain your answer.

Barbarossa: The German Invasion of Russia

Hitler believed Russia would be easily defeated. Why was he so mistaken? Why was this such a crucial error of judgement?

'The world will hold its breath ... '

'When Barbarossa commences the world will hold its breath,' Hitler said of his bold plan to invade the Soviet Union. The scale of the campaign was certainly huge. Hitler assembled three million troops, 3500 tanks and 2700 aircraft for 'Operation Barbarossa' – the German code-name for the attack on Russia.

Hitler invaded the Soviet Union on 22 June 1941, ordering his troops to flatten Russia 'like a hailstorm'. The reasons for the invasion were a mixture of the military and the political. Hitler needed Russia's plentiful **raw materials** to support his army and population. There was oil in the Caucasus and wheat in the Ukraine.

But he was also obsessed by racial ideas. The Russians were an 'inferior' Slav race. They were fit only to be the slaves of the new German Empire he was creating. Hitler believed the Russians, because they were racial inferiors, would offer no real resistance to racially superior Germans. Russia's fertile plains could provide even more *Lebensraum* than Poland. Russia was also the heart of world communism and Hitler detested communists. The defeat of Russia would deal a fatal blow to the world communist movement.

The Russian army had done very badly during its brief war with Finland in the winter of 1939–40.

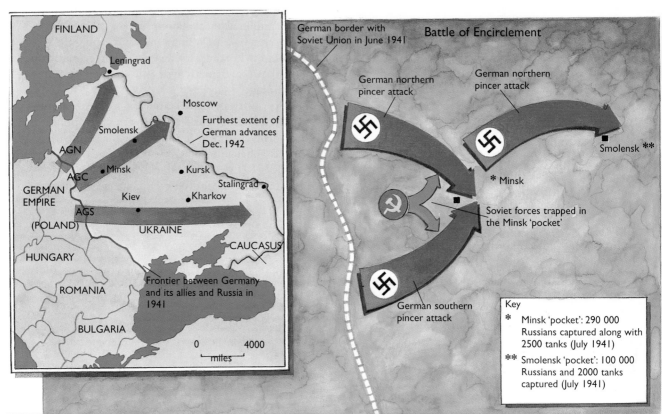

A Hitler believed that the French invasion of Russia in 1812 failed because they allowed the Russians to retreat. This drew the French deep into Russian territory and made it harder to keep their troops supplied. Hitler would stop the Russians retreating by getting *behind* the Soviet troops in 'battles of encirclement'. This would cut off their retreat and lead to the capture of large numbers of enemy troops. To some extent this worked but the Russian army was not short of men.

ВСЯ НАДЕЖДА НА ТЕБЯ, КРАСНЫЙ ВОИН!

B Soviet posters of the period concentrated on patriotic and basic human emotions to encourage resistance to the invaders. Nazi brutality against the occupied populations made this a fairly easy task. This poster declares: 'Our hope is in you, Red Warrior', as helpless civilians caught behind German lines are executed. What emotions do you think this poster is designed to stir?

This convinced Hitler that the Soviet Union and its Red Army could be beaten in four months. His confidence was also boosted by the fact that in the late 1930s Stalin, the Soviet dictator, had shot 35 000 officers (43 per cent of all his officers) in the Red Army. Stalin believed that the army was plotting against him.

But the invasion of Russia was Hitler's biggest mistake of the war so far – especially with Britain still undefeated in the west. Germany was now committed to a war on two fronts. Hitler's arrogance and contempt for his enemies was to prove his most serious failing.

Hitler was confident that his army would match the Soviet army in size and would have much better equipment. He was broadly right. The Soviet army totalled some 5.4 million men – but only three million of these faced the German attack. The Russians also had a vast number of tanks (10 000) and aircraft (8000) available to resist the invasion but these were mostly outdated in design. For example, only 1500 of the tanks were capable of fighting the German tanks on equal terms.

'Scorched earth'

The Russians were taken completely by surprise by the German invasion and fell back, trading men and territory for time. As they retreated they 'scorched the earth', destroying everything which could provide food or shelter for the Germans.

The Germans captured tremendous numbers of Soviet troops – three million by the end of 1941. But Stalin made good the losses in men and materials. He had ordered some 1500 factories (80 per cent of industrial output) to be moved by rail far to the east, away from the fighting. Here these factories were quickly in production once more. However many tanks the Germans destroyed or men they captured, they still seemed to face an endless supply of both.

Hitler had three principal targets within the Soviet Union. Army Group North (AGN) was ordered to capture Leningrad, an important armaments industry centre; Army Group Centre (AGC) headed for the capital, Moscow; Army Group South (AGS) set out for the Ukraine. Only AGS took its objective. In the north, Leningrad was besieged for three years until January 1944 and was never taken. AGC came within 60 kilometres of the capital in December 1941 but was halted and then driven back.

> The Germans had no intention of feeding Russian civilians under their control. They expected millions to die.

1 Copy 'the battle of encirclement' map (source A) into your file or exercise book. Then complete it as follows:
   a) Draw another 'German southern pincer attack' arrow which meets up with the northern one to the east (or right) of Smolensk.
   b) Draw the symbol of communist Russia (the hammer and sickle) inside these pincers with arrows trying to 'break out' as in the Minsk pocket.
   c) Explain the idea behind Hitler's 'battles of encirclement'. How successful was it?
2 Hitler had three military reasons for believing that the Russians would be beaten easily. What were they?
3 Using the evidence in this chapter, write a 15–20 line report to Hitler at the end of 1941 discussing:
   a) the progress of Barbarossa; what has been achieved?
   b) possible future problems; what targets have not been met? Why?

German Defeat in Russia

Why was the Battle of Stalingrad so important for each side? Could the outcome of the invasion of Russia have been different if Hitler had treated the Russians differently?

Stalingrad: 'Not a step back'

Hitler did not give up on the Caucasus oilfields. In the summer of 1942 he planned an offensive to capture Stalingrad. This would protect the flank of his army as it drove southwards towards the Caucasus. Stalin told the defenders of Stalingrad: 'Not a step back'. For five months, until January 1943, every room of every floor of every building was fought over. In one three-day period in September 1942 the railway station changed hands 15 times.

By the end of November the 300 000 Germans inside Stalingrad, under the command of Paulus, were cut off and surrounded by Russian forces commanded by General Zhukov. Paulus asked for permission to break out to save his army but Hitler refused. Instead, he promised to keep Paulus' Sixth Army supplied by air with 300 tonnes of food and ammunition a day. In fact, Paulus' troops never got more than 70 tonnes. Eventually, the remaining 90 000 Germans, cut off and starving, were forced to surrender on 30 January.

It was the biggest German defeat of the war so far. The Battle of Stalingrad was important for strategic reasons – the Germans could not now capture the Caucasus oilfields. But its real importance lay in the boost it gave to Soviet (and Allied) morale. The German army could be beaten.

Kursk: Operation Citadel

The only significant attempt by the Germans to stop the Russian advance after Stalingrad was at Kursk. Hitler code-named this, the biggest battle of the entire war, 'Operation Citadel'.

The Battle of Kursk (5–16 July 1943), in the words of Richard Overy, 'tore the heart out of the German army'. German and Russian losses in men and machines were huge but the difference was the Russians could replace both easily. In August 1943 the Germans had just 2500 tanks on the whole of the Eastern Front while the Soviet Union had 8200.

Stalingrad and Kursk were the two decisive battles on the Eastern Front. The German siege of Leningrad ended in January 1944 when the Russians relieved the city. It had lasted 900 days and cost at least 800 000 civilian lives. By August 1944 not a single German soldier was left on Russian soil and by December the Soviet Red Army was ready to invade Germany itself.

A Two Russian snipers in winter camouflage uniforms. The Russians were much better prepared than the Germans for winter warfare.

Why did Barbarossa fail?

Hitler expected to capture most of Russia's factories in the early stages of the war and this would make sure of a German victory. But Russia was able to make up its losses in tanks and planes because Stalin had managed to move over 1500 factories out of the range of the Germans.

But there were other reasons too. Hitler's over-confidence also led him to invade without preparing for a winter campaign. The war would be over

Temperatures were so low in the winter that urine froze before it hit the ground.

before the winter, Hitler claimed. The Soviet forces were much better equipped for this. The Germans, starved and exposed to the cold by the 'scorched earth' policy, simply froze.

The German generals liked to claim after the war that they lost simply because the Russians had more of everything – tanks, planes and men. This misses the point. The real reason for the Soviet victory was the tremendous courage and patriotism of their troops. Hitler's racial theories could not accept that Slav 'sub-humans' could display such qualities.

B The Germans treated Soviet partisans without mercy. A slow death by hanging or, if they were lucky, a quicker death by shooting, was all they could expect.

German brutality towards the Soviet civilians they controlled also worked against them. This brutality was partly caused by Nazi racial ideas of German superiority. As a result, many civilians joined the 250 000 or so resistance fighters or partisans against the German occupiers. It is possible that many of the peoples of the Soviet Union, such as the Ukrainians, would have accepted German rule in place of communism – if the Germans had treated them well.

The Red Army had taken on 75 per cent of Germany's military power and won and could justly claim to have done the most to defeat Hitler. The Soviet army eliminated no fewer than 607 German divisions with six million Germans killed, wounded or captured. The British and Americans together defeated just 176 divisions.

C One of the things which most impressed many Germans about their enemies was their ability to suffer without complaining. This German account describes a group of Soviet prisoners:

> Among the prisoners were wounded … One of them had his lower jaw torn away by a bullet and this wound he had bandaged roughly. Through the rags his windpipe, laid bare, was visible …
>
> Not one of them was moaning as they sat there in the grass … Why did they not moan? … But this was not all; a half dozen men who had been lying on the ground went forward pressing back into their bodies with their left hands intestines which had burst through the gaping wounds in their stomach wall … and not one of them cried … none moaned.

D Many Russians did choose to fight *with* the Germans as members of special SS squads. One of these describes a German raid on a Russian village:

> The people ran out of their houses, there was crying and screaming … I could see quite clearly about 50 women, old men and children – some of whom were babes in arms … I clearly saw some of the soldiers grabbing the people and throwing them into the well … The SS men shot at people from point-blank range … Some of them were killed on the spot, some wounded … The SS men began throwing corpses and wounded people, including children, into the well … We then burned the village down.

1 Why were the German defenders in Stalingrad doomed after November 1942?
2 Why was the victory at Stalingrad so important for the Russians?
3 a) How useful do you think sources B, C and D are to a historian studying the reasons for Germany's defeat in Russia? Comment on each source.
   b) Source C is a German account about Soviet prisoners. Does this mean you shouldn't believe it? Explain your answer.
4 Which reason for Germany's defeat do you think was the most important? Explain your answer.
5 'If the Germans had treated the occupied Soviet population better, they would have won the war on the Eastern Front.' Using the sources and text in Chapters 8 and 9, explain whether you agree or disagree with this interpretation.

From the Normandy Landings to Berlin

Why was it so important for the Allies to open up a 'Second Front? Why were the Normandy Landings successful?

The Second Front: June 1944

Stalin repeatedly asked Churchill and Roosevelt (the President of the USA) to open a **Second Front** by invading German-occupied France. This, he calculated, would force the Germans to withdraw troops from the war against Russia to deal with the British and Americans in France.

Stalin had expected the invasion of France to take place in 1943 but Churchill insisted that the attack be postponed for a year. Churchill told Stalin that an invasion of Italy had to come first. This, he claimed, would force the Germans to draw troops away from France to defend Italy. This would make an attack on France later on less

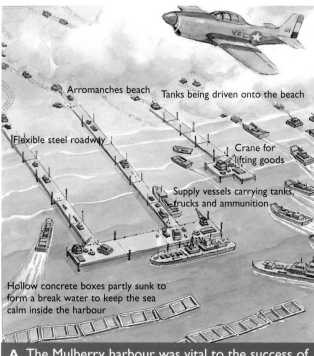

Arromanches beach

Tanks being driven onto the beach

Flexible steel roadway

Crane for lifting goods

Supply vessels carrying tanks, trucks and ammunition

Hollow concrete boxes partly sunk to form a break water to keep the sea calm inside the harbour

A The Mulberry harbour was vital to the success of the Normandy Landings. Here can be seen the flexible steel roadways onto which the heavy trucks and tanks were unloaded. The breakwater on the outside (half sunk concrete blocks) ensured that the water in the harbour would be calm.

difficult. Stalin suspected that the British and Americans really wanted the Russians to carry on killing Germans for them while Britain and the USA did very little. Relations between the three Allied powers were very strained at this time.

'Let's go!'

Eventually, after much secret planning, General Eisenhower, the American commander of all the Allied forces, decided that the good weather expected for 6 June 1944 would last long enough for a seaborne invasion of France to take place. D-Day would be 6 June. (The 'D', by the way, stands for 'Day'. The French call it 'Le Jour-J'.) He gave the go-ahead for Operation Overlord with the simple instruction: 'Let's go'.

The choice of the Normandy beaches took the Germans completely by surprise – there was no suitable port on the Normandy coast for the Allies to unload the huge amount of supplies and equipment they would need for an invasion. Therefore, the Germans – Field Marshall Rommel included – expected an attack across the shortest sea route to Calais.

What the Germans didn't know was that the Allies planned to bring their own 'ports' with them: a secret weapon called 'Mulberry'. These were artificial harbours which could be towed across the Channel, and onto which tanks, trucks and supplies could be unloaded. Even after the first landings had taken place Hitler was convinced that Normandy was not the real invasion. He held back two nearby tank divisions (over 500 tanks) until it was too late. When he was ready to use them, the British, American and Canadian divisions had established a firm hold on French soil.

60 000 troops landed on the first day and within a week over 300 000 were in France. After three months the number had grown to two million men and 450 000 vehicles pitched against the 600 000 troops available to Hitler. A key factor in the successful invasion was that the Germans had only 300 aircraft to use against the landings –

> The Germans were taken completely by surprise by the landing in Normandy. They believed the water was much too shallow.

NORWAY/
FINLAND
240 000
(19 Divisions)

NORWAY/
FINLAND
240 000
(19 Divisions)

FINLAND

SWEDEN

NORWAY

ESTONIA
Smolensk

LATVIA

LITHUANIA

GREAT
BRITAIN

NETHERLANDS

USSR

BELGIUM

GERMANY

POLAND

NW EUROPE
700 000
(58 Divisions)

LUX.

(CZECHO-
SLOVAKIA)

RUSSIAN FRONT
2 000 000
(160 Divisions)

SWITZER-
LAND

(AUSTRIA)

HUNGARY

Odessa

FRANCE

ITALY
300 000
(23 Divisions)

YUGOSLAVIA

ROMANIA

SPAIN

Rome

BALKANS
250 000
(20 Divisions)

BULGARIA

ALBANIA

GREECE

TURKEY

Allied to Germany or
under German occupation

Neutral State

Allied power or area
liberated by the Allies

B In 1944 German forces were spread across the continent of Europe. They were faced with a war on too many fronts.

compared with the 12 000 available to the Allies. From then onwards the Germans were gradually driven back towards Germany itself. Further bad news for Hitler arrived from Romania in August 1944. The Romanians changed sides, and abandoned their German allies. The Romanians had provided Germany with 23 per cent of its oil supplies and now this was lost.

There were only two setbacks to the Allies' progress: Arnhem (September 1944) and the Ardennes Offensive (December 1944). At Arnhem, Montgomery's plan was to use airborne troops to seize vital bridges in Holland *behind* the German lines. These would be essential later for the invasion of northern Germany. But the reinforcements failed to fight their way through and the attack collapsed. The losses at one of the bridges at Arnhem were especially severe. Of the 10 000 troops used here 8000 were killed or captured.

Hitler launched one last desperate counter-attack on the Belgian border in December to prevent an invasion of Germany itself. He used the last of his reserves and his fuel. At first, the Battle of the Bulge, as it is also known, was very successful as the Allies were taken completely by surprise. But because the Allies had more troops and far more aircraft they eventually broke the

German offensive by the end of January 1945. By using these vital reserves in the west and not against the Russians, all Hitler had done was make it easier for the Red Army to conquer more of Germany – including Berlin.

In March 1945 the Allies crossed the Rhine into Germany from the west. In the following month the Russians took Berlin, the capital of Nazi Germany. Hitler shot himself on 30 April – two days after Mussolini had been executed by Italian communist partisans. Mussolini's body was left hanging upside down from a Milan garage. On 8 May Germany **surrendered unconditionally**. Hitler had boasted that Nazism would last 1000 years – 12 had proved more than enough.

The Holocaust

The end of the war came too late for some six million Jews, victims of Hitler's Holocaust. This was the deliberate extermination of Europe's Jews. It was the result of Hitler's obsession with creating a '**master race**' (*Herrenvolk*) of Germanic peoples. He nearly succeeded. From 1942 onwards Himmler, the chief of the SS, organised the 'Final Solution' by shooting or gassing those Jews who were of no immediate use to the Nazis as slave labour. So efficient was this policy that, for instance, only 50 000 of Poland's 2.7 million Jews survived the war.

The SS did not rely on just Germans to carry out this policy. Many Poles, French and Russians in areas under Nazi control helped to identify and round up Jews for their German masters. The British authorities in the German-occupied Channel Islands co-operated with German laws concerning Jews. Anti-Semitism – the hatred and persecution of Jews – was not something in which only Germans believed.

1 Why was Stalin so keen on the Second Front?
2 Why were relations between Britain, the USA and Russia strained over the issue of the Second Front?
3 Does source B support Stalin's claim that the Russians – even after the landings in Normandy – were doing the bulk of the fighting against Germany?
Explain your answer.
4 Does source B suggest that Churchill's idea behind invading Italy had achieved its purpose? Explain your answer.

How Effective Was the Bombing of Germany?

How successful was the bombing of German cities in weakening the German war effort? Did the civilian population lose heart?

Strategic bombing

There were two types of bombing in the Second World War: strategic bombing and tactical bombing. Tactical bombing is the use of aircraft to bomb targets as part of an attack by the navy or the army. Strategic bombing involves attacks on the enemy's factories and cities.

When war broke out the Prime Minister at the time, Neville Chamberlain, ordered the RAF not to bomb Germany at all. He was afraid of provoking German raids on Britain. But Churchill had different ideas. He believed that strategic bombing was the only method Britain had of hitting back at Germany. He also faced a great deal of pressure from Stalin. Stalin had accused Britain of not doing enough in the fight against Nazism and Churchill had to offer something. He ordered the RAF's Bomber Command to launch an all-out bombing offensive over Germany. This was despite evidence from a British investigation in May 1942 which said that only 25 per cent of bombs dropped fell within *eight* kilometres of the target.

'Bomber' Harris

Arthur Harris became the commander of the RAF's Bomber Command in February 1942. He firmly believed that the war could be won by intensive bombing of Germany's cities. From 1942 onwards 'Bomber' Harris put his theories into practice – on Churchill's orders. In May 1942 he launched the first 1000-bomber raid over Germany with Cologne the target. This one raid killed about 40 000 Germans, and a week-long raid over Hamburg in July and August 1943 killed 45 000.

About 750 000 German civilians perished as a result of the RAF's night-time and the American day-time raids over Germany's cities. This is far more than the 60 000 Britons killed by German raids.

It has been a matter of some controversy whether these raids really did help defeat Germany. The historian, Richard Overy, has argued that the real success of the bombing offensive was that it forced the Germans to use valuable military resources (such as fighter planes) and men in defending their cities. In 1944, for example, one-third of all artillery pieces made were used as anti-aircraft guns. These guns would otherwise have been used against Allied tanks in France or Russia.

Arthur Harris, though, was ignored by Churchill at the end of the war. He was not made a lord, unlike the other war leaders, and there was no special medal for Bomber Command air crew. Harris was disgusted at this 'insult' and left England. It was not until 1995 that a statue was finally put up in his memory.

A This British poster from 1940 is clear that the RAF bombing campaign over Germany's cities is devastating German industry. Do the statistics in source G support this claim?

B This German poster of 1943 tries hard to bring home the message that lighted windows attract bombs. The German here says 'The enemy can spot your light! Black out your windows!'. 750 000 German civilians were killed by Allied raids.

C Arthur Harris, Commander in Chief of Bomber Command, addressed bomber crews in 1942 with these words:

It has been decided that the primary object of your operations should now be focused on the morale of the enemy civil population and, in particular, of the industrial workers … We are bombing Germany city by city and ever more terribly in order to make it impossible for her to go on with the war.

D A modern historian writes about the Allied bombing campaign over Germany (adapted from *Total War* by P Calvocoressi, 1972):

In Berlin the damage was severe enough to cause many to leave the city and to close all the schools, but less than half of the city's industries stopped work and many of the stoppages were brief … morale did not break in either Berlin or Hamburg. Bomber Command failed to bring German industry to a halt.

E Brigadier Peter Young gives a different picture (from *World War 1939–45*, 1966):

On October 14, 1943, 291 US Flying Fortresses set off to attack the greatest centre of German ball-bearing production. The Fortresses did severe damage but 60 were shot down. The strategic bombing offensive brought the German war economy almost to the point of collapse.

F Another view is provided by the historian A N Frankland (from *The Oxford Companion to the Second World War*, 1995):

British Bomber Command and the Eighth USAAF [United States Army Air Force] did produce an oil famine in Germany, the collapse of its transport system and a fearful levelling of its great cities. These results were too late to win the war on their own, but they did make a decisive contribution to the defeat of Germany.

G Statistics of German industrial and military output from 1940–44 with industrial output shown in millions of tonnes.

	1940	1941	1942	1943	1944
Coal	268	315	318	340	348
Steel	21	28	29	31	26
Oil	5	6	7	8	5
Tanks	2200	5200	9200	17 300	22 100
Aircraft	10 200	11 800	15 400	24 800	39 800

1 Harris identified two basic aims for Bomber Command in source C. The first was to destroy the morale of the civilian population and especially its industrial workers. What was the second?

2 In what way does source C support source A as far as the aims of Bomber Command are concerned?

3 What does Calvocoressi in source D say about whether these aims were achieved?

4 How does Brigadier Young in source E disagree with Calvocoressi? Which of Bomber Command's aims doesn't Young comment on?

5 Frankland in source E claims that the bombing produced an 'oil famine' in Germany. Does source G support this in your view?

6 Go through each of sources D, E and F and point out where, if at all, the statistics in source G lend support to the views in the sources or where they contradict them.

7 'The bombing of Germany had no significant impact on Germany's ability or will to fight.' Using sources A to G and your own knowledge, comment on whether you agree or disagree with this interpretation.

The War in the Atlantic

Why was it vital to keep shipping routes open? How close did the Germans come to winning the 'Battle of the Atlantic'?

The Atlantic lifeline

Britain in 1939 imported half its food and two-thirds of its raw materials. The Atlantic Ocean soon became a battleground as Britain fought to keep the seas safe for its merchant ships to bring in these vital supplies. The main threat came from German U-boats or submarines. Submarines were very small craft but each one of their 14 torpedoes could sink any ship afloat.

Germany's U-boat or submarine fleet was led by Admiral Doenitz but at the start of the war he had only 22 U-boats available for use in the Atlantic. The period 1940–41 was, nonetheless, very successful for the U-boats, especially as their numbers increased. In 1941 Britain only managed to import 26 million tonnes of supplies – compared with the 68 million tonnes needed in 1938. By January 1942 Doenitz had a U-boat fleet of 300.

About one third of a torpedo was taken up by oxygen for the engine.

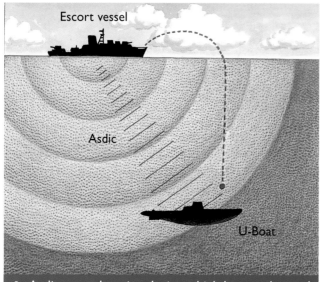
Escort vessel

Asdic

U-Boat

A Asdic was a locating device which bounced sound off solid objects, such as a U-boat hull. The time between sending and getting back the signal gave the position of the target. Other listening devices could detect a submarine from the noise of its electric motor – until the Germans developed quieter motors.

Anti-submarine methods

The British quickly adopted the convoy system of escorting merchant ships with anti-submarine warships called destroyers. Destroyers used an electronic listening device called sonar or asdic which detected the position of submerged U-boats. The destroyer then fired off several depth charges (underwater explosive devices). These were set to explode at a fixed depth. The pressure of the explosion could crush or split a submarine's hull but it had to be close enough – no more than nine metres away.

Submarines on the surface used diesel engines but below the surface they could only use battery-powered electric motors. After a day, the air in the cramped quarters became unbreathable and they would have to surface. This is when they were most at risk from being spotted by aircraft and enemy ships.

From 1943 submarines weren't even safe at night. This was because the invention of centimetric radar allowed aircraft and ships to detect a surfaced submarine in the dark up to six kilometres away. They were then able to use a powerful searchlight equal to 80 million candles to pinpoint its precise position.

The Germans partly managed to get round this problem by using a snorkel pipe which reached the surface from periscope depth. This allowed in enough air to run the diesel engines below the water. But these weren't in use until early 1944 and by then it was too late to bring the U-boats victory in the 'Battle of the Atlantic'.

'The happy times'

Despite such anti-submarine methods the U-boat threat was extremely serious. Doenitz ordered his submarines to attack in large groups of 'wolf packs' at night and on the surface where they could not be detected by sonar. This proved very effective and Britain lost 1875 ships in 1940 and 1941 in the Atlantic – a quarter of Britain's merchant fleet. The German crews called these years 'the happy times'.

East coast carnage

In December 1941 the USA entered the war and the 'happy times' of 1941 became even happier. The Americans decided against the convoy system

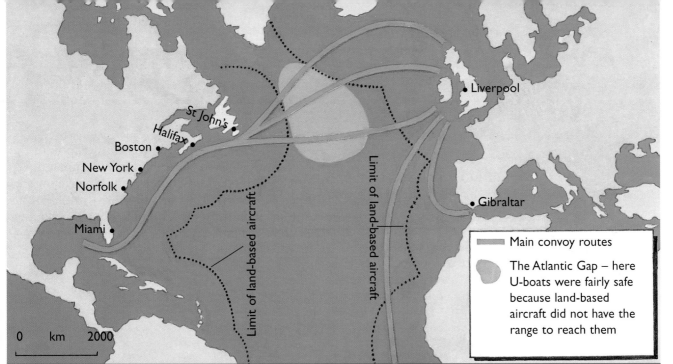

Liverpool
St John's
Halifax
Boston
New York
Norfolk
Miami
Gibraltar

Limit of land-based aircraft
Limit of land-based aircraft

0   km   2000

Main convoy routes

The Atlantic Gap – here
U-boats were fairly safe
because land-based
aircraft did not have the
range to reach them

B Up to 1943 the German U-boats had been able to operate fairly safely in what was called 'the Atlantic Gap'. This was a stretch of about 1000 km in the middle of the Atlantic which land-based aircraft could not reach. But from early in 1943 long-range aircraft equipped with centimetric radar could fly over this area with devastating effect. In May alone Doenitz lost 46 U-boats. 237 U-boats were sunk in the Atlantic in 1943 – 149 of them by aircraft. The Battle of the Atlantic was over.

and their merchant ships sailed unescorted, close to the east coast of the USA. At night the ships could be seen against the lights of the coastal cities and were easy prey for the U-boat packs of 15–20 submarines. The authorities were against a blackout because it would be bad for tourism! In May 1942 the Americans ordered a blackout on the east coast and began to organise convoy escorts for their merchant ships.

The end of the 'U-boat peril'

Over six million tonnes of British and American shipping were sunk in 1942 (nearly 1200 ships) and by January 1943 the Royal Navy had only two months' supply of oil left. 'The only thing that ever really frightened me in the whole war,' wrote Churchill later, 'was the U-boat peril'. But by the end of 1943 the 'U-boat peril' had been beaten.

The Allies built 14 million tonnes of new ships in 1943. U-boat losses had become too high for the Germans – between August and December 1943 only 51 ships were sunk in the Atlantic in a year in which the Germans lost 237 submarines. Only 117 ships were sunk in the whole of 1944. The Germans built 1100 submarines during the war. 785 of these were sunk and 28 000 of Germany's U-boat crews (72 per cent of the total) perished with them.

C Allied merchant ships sunk in the Atlantic, 1939–44:

	Tonnes	Number of ships
1939	755 000	220
1940	3 650 000	1007
1941	3 300 000	875
1942	6 150 000	1170
1943	2 170 000	363
1944	500 000	117

1 Why was the Atlantic so important to Britain?
2 What problems did submarines face in terms of:
   a) submarine technology?
   b) enemy measures against them?
3 Look at source C. What was the average tonnage of a merchant ship in (i) 1940 and (ii) 1944? (You get this by dividing the amount of tonnage sunk by the number of ships sunk.) What conclusion can you reach from this?
4 1943 was the decisive year in the Battle of the Atlantic.
   a) How does source C support this?
   b) What reasons can you find in the text to explain this success for the Allies?

Why Did Germany Lose the War?

Were the Allies better equipped? Does bigger industrial production alone explain the Allied victory?

A glance at the statistics in source D suggests an easy answer to this question. The Germans lost because of the Allies' huge industrial power. This meant that the Allies could produce vast quantities of weapons and that they had the ability to keep these weapons going.

A One German commander at Normandy was well aware of what the Allied industrial power meant:

> I cannot understand these Americans. Each night we know that we have cut them to pieces, inflicted heavy casualties, mowed down their transport. But – in the morning, we are suddenly faced with fresh troops, with complete replacements of men, machines, food, tools and weapons. This happens every day.

Hitler claimed he lost the war because of the alliance with Italy – 'Anything would have been better than having the Italians as allies'. This alliance drew German forces into the Mediterranean when they should have been concentrating on Russia. Hitler also claimed that a two-front war against Britain and Russia was a big factor in Germany's defeat.

But Germany never had more than 20 divisions operating in the Mediterranean during the war – whereas over 600 were eliminated by the Russians between 1941 and 1945. The USA fought a three-front war which was many thousands of kilometres from its shores and still won.

German ill-treatment of the people they conquered has also been put forward as a reason for their defeat. The chapters on the war in Russia suggest that some of the Soviet peoples were ready to support Germany rather than communism but they soon turned against Germany. As many as 250 000 Soviet partisans fought the Germans behind their lines, tying down many troops. Similar resistance groups sprang up in Poland, France and Italy.

Aircraft: the key to victory

Historians, though, place much more importance on the industrial power of the British, Americans and Russians. This allowed the Allies to produce vast numbers of the most important weapon of the war: aircraft. The strategic bombing campaign over Germany tied up 80 per cent of Germany's fighter planes in 1944. Air superiority in the D-Day Landings meant the Allies had a 70 to 1 advantage over the Germans in planes.

B At first the Germans were able to win the support of considerable numbers of men within the countries they occupied. They were willing to join them in the fight against the communist Soviet Union. Such men enlisted in the Waffen SS which was made up of foreigners fighting with the Germans.

C This striking American poster from 1943 clearly gives one reason why the Allies were fighting – to save Christian civilisation from the evil of the Axis. The fact that the Allies believed, rightly, that they were fighting to free the world from a monstrous evil is an important factor in explaining their victory.

In August 1944 Romania quit the war and Germany lost 23 per cent of its oil supplies. Germany had so little oil left in 1944 that producing more tanks and planes would have been pointless anyway – they couldn't have moved. All of this suggests that Germany was doomed to lose the war – at least once the USA joined in. But overwhelming industrial power doesn't always lead to victory in war. The United States found this out 30 years later when it lost the Vietnam War. It is not enough to have more of everything. It is vital to have the will to win as well.

D A comparison of German and Allied industrial and military production in 1944:

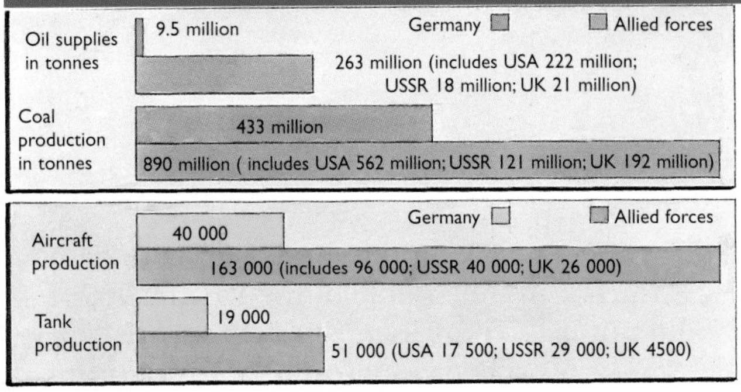

	Germany ☐	Allied forces ☐
Oil supplies in tonnes	9.5 million	263 million (includes USA 222 million; USSR 18 million; UK 21 million)
Coal production in tonnes	433 million	890 million (includes USA 562 million; USSR 121 million; UK 192 million)

	Germany ☐	Allied forces ☐
Aircraft production	40 000	163 000 (includes 96 000; USSR 40 000; UK 26 000)
Tank production	19 000	51 000 (USA 17 500; USSR 29 000; UK 4500)

Q

1 What reason does source A suggest for Germany's defeat?
2 How convincing do you find Hitler's reasons for Germany's defeat? Explain your answer.
3 Which group of the statistics quoted in source D do you think was the most important in helping to achieve an Allied victory? Give reasons for your answer.
4 Copy the chart below into your file or book. Then complete the empty columns by commenting on why the reasons given were important and not so important in deciding why Germany lost. A couple of examples have been done for you.

Extended writing
Write about 300 words on the following question: 'Germany was bound to lose the war the moment the United States joined the war.' Explain whether you agree or disagree with this interpretation by using the text and sources in this and earlier chapters.

Reason for defeat of Germany	This reason is important because ...	This reason is not so important because ...
1 Germany could not match the Allies' industrial production in coal and oil.		
2 The Germans over-committed themselves by fighting on too many fronts. (See also source A in Chapter 10.)	The Germans committed large numbers of troops to fronts in France, Italy and the Soviet Union. They didn't have the resources to do this.	
3 The Allied bombing offensive over Germany created another 'front' which took up valuable resources which the Germans needed elsewhere. (See also Chapter 11.)		
4 Germany had a lower output of military equipment for planes and tanks.		
5 German ill-treatment of occupied peoples led to resistance groups being formed. (See also Chapters 7, 8 and 9.)		Resistance groups only had a limited effect on the German war effort and weren't active until Germany had already begun to lose the war.

Pearl Harbor

Why were the Americans taken by surprise?

The Japanese attack on the American naval base at Pearl Harbor in the middle of the Pacific Ocean should not have come as a complete surprise to the Americans. The Japanese and the Americans were the two great Pacific powers who competed with each other to dominate the region. The United States was content with dominating the region economically but the Japanese wanted to control South East Asia by conquering it.

Conflict with the United States seemed inevitable – especially after the Americans imposed a ban or boycott on the sale of oil to Japan in July 1941. The Americans imposed the boycott because Japan had invaded China in 1937. This was a severe blow to the Japanese economy since they depended on the USA for two-thirds of their oil supplies.

The military leaders realised that Japan could never dominate South East Asia unless it controlled its own supplies of vital raw materials like oil, rubber, iron ore and rice. These could only be acquired through war. If Japan was to stand any chance in a war against the USA it would have to strike first with a devastating blow. They chose the American Pacific Fleet at Pearl Harbor in Hawaii as the target.

Pearl Harbor

American intelligence had cracked the Japanese secret code. They knew that an attack against the United States was planned – only they were not sure where. It was assumed the target would be the Philippines and not Pearl Harbor.

If war broke out, the American commander of the Pacific Fleet, Admiral Kimmel, was under orders to prepare to attack the Japanese Marshall Islands. These were 3250 kilometres to the *south west* of Pearl Harbor. This was the area which Kimmel kept an eye on with the three reconnaissance planes he had. But the Japanese attack, when it came, came from the *north* and Kimmel was taken completely by surprise.

Kimmel didn't think Pearl Harbor could be attacked by torpedoes dropped by planes because the water in the harbour wasn't deep enough for them. So he removed the nets which protected the ships from torpedoes. What the Americans didn't

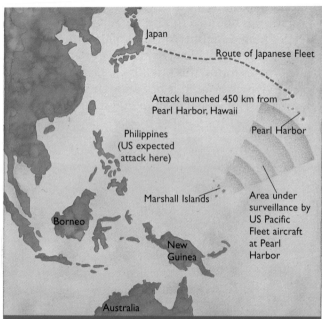

A Pearl Harbor was a long way from Japan and the United States thought any attack would be much closer to Japan itself – probably the Philippines. The Americans had plans to attack the Japanese Marshall Islands if war broke out.

know was that the Japanese had changed their torpedoes to run in shallow water. These were the same type of torpedoes the British had used against the Italian fleet 13 months earlier.

Kimmel was afraid that Japanese agents in Hawaii might try sabotage against Pearl Harbor's aircraft. So these were grouped together to make it easier to guard them. When the Japanese fleet sailed undetected 5500 kilometres across the Pacific to within 450 kilometres of Hawaii, the Americans were looking elsewhere. Two waves of Japanese aircraft pounded the Pacific fleet of 70 ships in its harbour on Sunday morning, 7 December 1941.

Carriers escape!

Six battleships were sunk plus ten other ships and 164 planes destroyed. 2400 servicemen and civilians also died. However, though the damage was devastating, it was not as great as the Japanese had hoped. The American aircraft carriers – a key target – were out on manoeuvres that morning.

Furthermore, the Japanese commander, Nagumo, decided not to attack the ship repair facilities or the oil storage units. This meant the damaged vessels could be repaired quickly and the fleet had the fuel to hit back – when it was ready. But that would not be for another six months.

In the long term, Pearl Harbor was not a success for the Japanese. The attack enraged American public opinion because it came *before* an official declaration of war. If Japan had occupied Pearl Harbor and seized for itself the vast oil supplies there, things may have turned out differently. All Admiral Yamamoto's bold plan really achieved was to delay for six months the full impact of America's anger.

The Japanese chose a Sunday morning to attack Pearl Harbor because they knew many of the American servicemen would have been out on the town the night before.

B The fact that the Japanese attack was carried out *before* a declaration of war united and enraged the American people. This poster was designed to remind Americans of what President Roosevelt called a 'day of infamy'.

D Another historian, William Manchester, wrote this about Admiral Kimmel at Pearl Harbor (adapted from *Goodbye Darkness*, 1979):

US commanders in Hawaii and the Philippines were told '… an aggressive move by Japan is expected in the next few days'. The admiral at Pearl Harbor decided to take no precautions. So officers and men were given their usual Saturday evening off on December 6. Only 195 of the navy's 780 anti-aircraft guns in the harbour were manned. And most of them lacked ammunition. It had been returned to storage because it tended to 'get dusty'.

C On 6 December, the day before Pearl Harbor was attacked, an American intelligence official decoded a top secret Japanese message. This extract outlines events:

The message was shown to President Roosevelt, who said: 'This means war'. Even so, no warning was sent to Hawaii where the Pacific Fleet was based. In fact, no Japanese decoded messages had been sent to the fleet's commander, Admiral Kimmel, for months … Two months earlier, SIS, the US Army Signal Intelligence Service, had decoded a message from Tokyo to the Japanese consul on Hawaii. The message divided the waters of Pearl Harbor into five areas and asked for the exact locations of Kimmel's warships and carriers. Both Army and Navy intelligence officers in Washington guessed this could be a grid system for a bombing attack. Several of these men urged that Kimmel … be warned but for some reason their superiors would not allow this.

1 Why were the Japanese and the Americans likely to come into conflict with each other?
2 Why was war between the two more likely after July 1941?
3 Give three reasons why the Japanese attack was not as successful as it could have been.
4 Why, according to source C, could Kimmel feel let down by the government and the intelligence services?
5 What are the differences between sources C and D regarding who was responsible for the disaster at Pearl Harbor?
6 Kimmel was found guilty of failing to do his duty while in command at Pearl Harbor and was sacked from the navy. Imagine you are the lawyer either defending or prosecuting him and write 100–150 words summarising your argument at his 'trial'.

The United States Strikes Back

How did the United States fight back? Was the dropping of atomic bombs on Japan necessary to get it to surrender?

For six months after Pearl Harbor, Japan had a free hand in the Pacific and in South East Asia. It launched attacks at the same time against the British in Burma and Malaya. Here there were vital raw materials: oil and rubber. Japanese troops rolled back the British, Australians and Americans as victory followed victory. Singapore was Britain's key naval base in the Far East. Its loss in February 1942 along with 62 000 prisoners was a huge blow to morale.

Midway: turning point

The spectacular run of Japanese victories came to an end with the Battle of Midway in June 1942. The Japanese planned to seize the United States island of Midway. But the Americans knew of the plan, because they had deciphered Japan's secret code. The Americans ambushed the enemy's fleet and sank four aircraft carriers for the loss of just one United States carrier.

The loss of these four aircraft carriers proved to be devastating because Japan managed to build only another seven in the next two years. In the same time the United States built 90.

'Withering on the vine'

The Americans took command of the Allied campaign in the Pacific. General MacArthur would advance by land from the South West Pacific area and Admiral Nimitz by sea across the Pacific Ocean. The Americans developed an 'island hopping' or 'leapfrogging' strategy. This was similar to Hitler's *Blitzkrieg* in that strongly defended enemy islands were bypassed and isolated from support and reinforcements.

These well-defended islands were, in MacArthur's memorable phrase, 'left to wither on the vine'. This limited American casualties and speeded up their progress across the vast distances and hundreds of islands held by the Japanese. In one spectacular move in 1944 MacArthur 'hopped' 930 kilometres to seize a Japanese base and in doing so bypassed 40 000 enemy troops.

The United States' Pacific progress, nonetheless, proved to be costly. Japanese resistance was fanatical. The warrior code of *bushido* taught that capture in battle was shameful. Japanese soldiers, therefore, preferred to fight to the death. Iwo Jima, a tiny volcanic island, was defended by 23 000 Japanese troops. Of these 22 000 fought to the death rather than surrender.

Other Japanese volunteered for *kamikaze* suicide missions (*kamikaze* means 'divine wind'). From October 1944 onwards over 5000 pilots flew their planes packed with explosives against American

A American land forces under MacArthur and naval forces under Nimitz planned to advance on Okinawa. From here they could invade Japan.

JAPAN

June 1945: Okinawa captured. Invasion of Japan by sea now possible

○ Major Battles

June 1942: US victory forces Japan out of the Central Pacific

June 1944: US control Marianas Islands and can now bomb Japan

Okinawa

Pearl Harbor

Philippine Sea

PHILIPPINES

ADMIRAL NIMITZ

Leyte Gulf

Dec. 1941: Attack by Japan brings US into war

GENERAL MACARTHUR

BORNEO

NEW GUINEA

Oct. 1944: Philippines re-conquered. Japan cut off from oil supplies in Dutch East Indies

AUSTRALIA

B These American prisoners are about to set out on the 'March of Death' in April 1942. In general, 27 per cent of American prisoners died in Japanese hands. Statistics like these show how the war in the Pacific was even more ferocious than the one in Europe.

ships. One volunteer was turned down because he was married with a wife and three young daughters. The wife drowned herself and her daughters so that he could carry out his mission. It was this kind of devotion to their Emperor, Hirohito, which so worried the Americans. What would American casualties be like when they had to attack Japan itself – and not tiny islands thousands of kilometres away?

From the Marianas to Okinawa

In June 1944 the biggest carrier battle of the war, the Battle of the Philippine Sea, saw an American victory. This allowed them to occupy the Marianas Islands. From one of these, Saipan, the US Army Air Force could now bomb Japan itself. In October 1944 Japan suffered another crucial defeat at the Battle of Leyte Gulf.

This led, four months later, to the reconquest of the Philippines by MacArthur which cut off Japan from its oil supplies in the Dutch East Indies. The loss of 60 million barrels of a oil a year was a crushing blow to a country which could produce only two million barrels of its own. These barrels represented 80 per cent of Japan's total oil supply.

The capture of Okinawa took place in June 1945 after two months of vicious fighting. 13 000 American soldiers and sailors had died to capture an island 550 kilometres from Japan itself. From here an invasion of mainland Japan could at last be launched – but at what cost to the United States?

The atomic bombing of Japan

On 6 August the Americans dropped the world's first atomic bomb on Hiroshima and followed it three days later with another on Nagasaki. These two bombs killed over 200 000 people between them, many dying months later from the effects of radiation. The day after the bombing of Nagasaki, 10 August, Japan agreed to surrender.
It is generally assumed that the bombs forced Japan to surrender. Recent evidence suggests otherwise. After all, the American fire-bombing of Tokyo on one night in March 1945 had killed 85 000 civilians and the government of Japan fought on. Civilian casualties, therefore, were probably not an issue.

It is true that American lives were saved because a full-scale invasion of Japan was not needed but this was not because of the two atomic bombs. Japan agreed to surrender because President Truman dropped the United States demand for **unconditional surrender**. The Japanese would surrender, they said, if Emperor Hirohito were allowed to stay on the throne.

Truman agreed to this one condition and the war was over. He could have agreed to it *before* the bombing but then the awesome power of the weapon would not have been proved. By demonstrating it, the United States delivered a timely warning to the Soviet Union not to cause problems with the Western powers after the war.

1 Why was 'island hopping' an appropriate strategy for the USA in the Pacific?
2 Why was the loss of the Philippines such a blow to Japan?
3 Why did the fierce resistance of Japanese troops on islands like Saipan worry the Americans so much?
4 The views of the historians in sources C and D about the importance of the atomic bombs are different.
   a) In what way are the two sources different?
   b) Is there anything in the provenance of these sources which explains this difference in interpretation? Explain your answer.
5 'The dropping of the atomic bombs on Japan was an unnecessary and brutal act.' What is your opinion of this view?

Why Was Japan Defeated?

Japanese troops were noted for their courage and unwillingness to surrender. Why then were they defeated?

Japan's gamble

Countries lose wars for a variety of reasons. Poor equipment, morale, and strategies can play a part as can lack of industrial resources. The Japanese knew very well that they couldn't match the huge industrial resources of the United States but the military leaders who led Japan into war didn't think this would matter. Their plan was simple. A surprise attack would allow Japan to conquer so much of the Pacific that the United States would be forced to negotiate a treaty. The Americans, the Japanese believed, would not have the stomach for the kind of casualties involved in a full-scale war to get these territories back.

However, it was a massive gamble because if the Japanese got the American response wrong they would surely lose the war. Japan's raw material resources were totally inadequate for a modern war. It depended on imports for 80 per cent of its iron ore and oil supplies. It had no bauxite (essential for electric cables and explosives) or rubber (essential for tyres).

Shortages

The people of Japan had no particular enthusiasm for war but they were excited by the early victories. The government could keep morale up at first because Japan was winning. Later, it kept secret news of defeats like Midway. But a military dictatorship like Japan can only keep defeats from the population for a time. Rationing gradually became more severe as Japan's already small merchant fleet was sunk by American submarines and supplies became desperately short.

The Japanese never really grasped the importance of the submarine as an economic weapon. This was one which could be used against an enemy's supplies by attacking its merchant fleet. Japan's small submarine fleet was used more and more to keep its faraway garrisons in the Pacific supplied. This became more of a problem because of MacArthur's 'island hopping' strategy. Isolated garrisons, bypassed by the fighting, still had to be kept fed. These submarines would have been better used attacking American merchant ships.

A Japanese '*kamikaze*' pilots pose before a suicide bombing attack on American ships. *Kamikaze* pilots were all volunteers and there was no shortage of them. Americans were prepared to die – if necessary – but the idea of deliberately killing yourself was something they found hard to understand. But for the Japanese, death in battle was an honour.

In 1941, Japan had to import two million tonnes of rice to feed its population but in 1944 it could only manage to import 650 000 tonnes. This was because 85 per cent of its merchant ships were sunk during the war. American bomber raids also helped to bring home to the population that Japan was losing the war. By February 1944 even the military leaders realised the war was lost.

B Japanese forces on various fronts in August 1943; figures are calculated on the estimate that each division is roughly 18 000 troops:	
Pacific	270 000 (15 divisions)
Manchuria	270 000 (15 divisions)
China	470 000 (26 divisions)
Burma	110 000 (6 divisions)
Korea	36 000 (2 divisions)

C A comparison of Japanese and Allied industrial and military production in 1944: note that the USSR has been left out of these tables because the Russians didn't declare war on Japan until August 1945. It's also worth remembering that Japan was only fighting Britain and the USA. The British and the Americans had to use their weapons and supplies for the war against Germany as well.

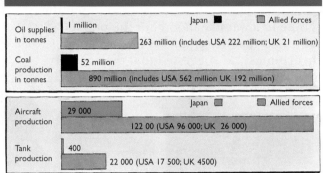

	Japan ▪	Allied forces ▪
Oil supplies in tonnes	1 million	263 million (includes USA 222 million; UK 21 million)
Coal production in tonnes	52 million	890 million (includes USA 562 million UK 192 million)

	Japan ▪	Allied forces ▪
Aircraft production	29 000	122 00 (USA 96 000; UK 26 000)
Tank production	400	22 000 (USA 17 500; UK 4500)

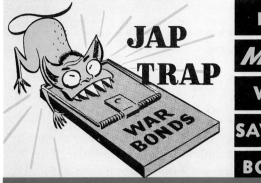

BUY *MORE* WAR SAVINGS BONDS

JAP TRAP — WAR BONDS

D American propaganda frequently showed the Japanese as various types of animals – apes, monsters, giant bats and rats (as in this poster). Sometimes they were shown as comic characters with huge buck teeth and glasses. This poster is urging Americans to lend the government money to support the war effort.

Q

Why Japan lost the war

Some general reasons for the defeat of Japan are put forward in the chart below. Your task is to copy the chart into your file and then find evidence to support these reasons (from the text and the sources) to enter in the second column. Then evaluate each reason in terms of its importance in causing the defeat of Japan. There isn't a right or wrong answer for this final part – the quality of your answer depends on how well you argue your case and the quality of the evidence you have to support it. An example has been done for you but you are welcome to improve on it!

Extended writing

Write about 300 words on the following question: 'Why were the Japanese so successful in the early stages of the war? Why, then, did Japan lose the war?'

You will find it useful to make use of some or all of the following points: the importance of Japan's surprise attack; morale and commitment of the Japanese forces; the economic and military strengths of both sides; over-commitment of the Japanese forces.

Reason for defeat of Japan	Evidence in the text sources	Importance of this reason in the Japanese defeat
1 Japan could not match the Allies' industrial production.		
2 The Japanese over-committed themselves by fighting on too many fronts.		
3 The Japanese forces depended on conquered territories for vital raw materials. As they retreated they lost these raw materials.	The loss of the Dutch East Indies cut Japan off from 80% of its oil supplies.	The loss of raw materials such as oil was a crippling blow to Japan since without adequate petrol supplies its armed forces were less and less effective.
4 Japan had a lower output of military equipment.		

The Propaganda War

Key Issues

How effective was British propaganda? What forms did it take?

When war broke out in September 1939 the mood of the British people was not enthusiastic. The feeling was more one of 'let's get it over with'. A Canadian poet, Milton Acorn, wrote these lines in 1939:

This is where we came in; this has happened before
Only the last time there was cheering.

The 'last time', of course, was the First World War of 1914-18. The population did cheer when war broke out in 1914 but not this time. The government, though, was better prepared for war in 1939. Air Raid Precautions (ARP) had begun in 1938 and there were 100 000 **air-raid wardens** ready for duty. **Conscription** had been started in April 1939 – five months before the war started.

Mass Observation

The British public's reluctance to fight another war seemed justified as defeat followed defeat. It was the job of the government to keep up morale and to keep a check on it. Mass Observation was an organisation whose members reported conversations they overheard in pubs, shops and elsewhere. They also interviewed members of the public about specific issues to do with the war. The Ministry of Information used these reports to keep in touch with the public mood.

Sometimes these reports were very critical of the government's efforts to keep up morale. After the fall of France in June 1940, public morale was very low and Mass Observation blamed the government's poor efforts over propaganda. Government propaganda, it said, failed to lift the spirits of the people because it was written by upper class people who didn't understand how ordinary people spoke or felt.

The Ministry of Information (MoI) was the government department responsible for keeping the public informed about their duties and for maintaining their support for the war. It decided from the start to avoid exaggerating victories. This was easy to do when the news was mostly bad until late 1942. It would also avoid playing down defeats. The MoI would try to get across the truth and not give the public false hopes of early victory. This was a sensible approach but the Ministry's early efforts were generally feeble and the public response was poor.

How not to design a poster

The Ministry of Information's first poster (see source A) was dismal and uninspiring – typical of other early efforts. It was supposed to put the people in a war-like mood but the public suspected that the emphasis on *Your* courage, *your* cheerfulness ...' suggested that the ordinary public would be making the sacrifices for the benefit of the upper classes.

YOUR COURAGE
YOUR CHEERFULNESS
YOUR RESOLUTION

WILL BRING US VICTORY

A This was a government official's idea of a stirring poster. Eventually, British posters would be designed by people who knew about effective propaganda but this was not one of them.

The public's feeling that the war was in the hands of people who didn't know what they were doing was strengthened by this ineffective kind of propaganda. On the other hand, German radio propaganda broadcasts by 'Lord Haw-Haw' were listened to regularly by six million Britons by January 1940. They believed that the government was keeping back from them the sort of information contained in these German broadcasts (which were also entertaining). Lord Haw-Haw, whose real name was William Joyce, was later executed by the British for treason – even though he was an American citizen.

Fifth Columnists

British poster propaganda was at its best when it appealed to the humour of the British people. Source B, from the MoI, shows one of a series of posters designed to stop people carelessly giving away military information to spies. The posters were popular and effective. There was a general worry that large numbers of German spies or British Nazi sympathisers, known as **Fifth Columnists**, were at work in Britain, listening in on careless conversations.

B 'Careless talk costs lives.' The threat from German spies listening in on conversations was rather exaggerated. All German spies in Britain were captured. Some became useful double agents and worked for Britain.

The government also urged members of the public to inform on people making **defeatist** comments. This campaign was not popular and it created a tense and suspicious atmosphere. Churchill ordered it to be stopped – though only after 70 000 German and Italian citizens living in Britain had been arrested in May 1940 as potential Fifth Columnists. Some of those arrested and **interned** were in fact men who had fled from Germany and Italy to escape fascism. By the summer of 1941, the Fifth Columnist scare had died down and only 5000 committed Nazis and fascists were still in internment camps.

Black propaganda

The Political Warfare Executive (PWE) was a government department which had the job of sending 'black propaganda' to the Germans. This type of propaganda involves the use of lies and trickery to undermine the morale of the enemy or confuse them. The PWE was particularly imaginative but it is hard to say how successful its ideas were. Among its activities was the operation of a secret radio transmitter.

About 90 per cent of what the PWE broadcast was true, giving accurate details of German victories and Allied defeats. The broadcasters claimed they were anti-Nazi Germans inside the German army but their reports were also anti-British. Broadcasters even described Churchill as 'that flat-footed bastard of a drunken old Jew'. This helped to convince Germans that the broadcast could not be British. Occasionally, an invented item would be slipped into the reports.

One example was when a PWE broadcast informed German servicemen of the names of German streets destroyed in a bombing raid the previous evening. These men were told that if they lived in one of these streets they could get special leave to visit their families. Of course, when they applied for permission to visit them they were told no leave was possible. This, the PWE hoped, would anger them and lower the morale of the German servicemen.

C Germans were not allowed to listen to foreign radio broadcasts, in this case from London and Moscow. Those who did were labelled traitors –'Verrater'. One of the phrases in the spiral of words coming from the foreign microphone is *Soldatensender* – the name of the PWE's propaganda broadcast to Germany.

1 In what ways was the government ready for war in 1939?
2 Why do you think there was no cheering when war broke out in 1939 while the people had cheered in 1914?
3 Can you suggest any reasons why source A was not a successful poster?
4 Do you think the order to arrest 70 000 Germans and Italians was (i) understandable and (ii) necessary? Think particularly about when the decision was made.
5 Do you think the PWE's fake radio programme would have been effective as propaganda? Give reasons for your answer.

The Blitz

What did the Blitz achieve? How did the civilian population and the rescue services cope? What was the state of morale in the country?

Until the end of August 1940 both sides in the war avoided bombing civilian targets. The RAF did bomb industrial areas, such as the Ruhr in Germany, in May and June of 1940 but the first RAF bombs did not fall on Berlin until the night of 24–25 August 1940. Hitler was so outraged by this raid that he immediately ordered Goering, the commander of the Luftwaffe, to begin reprisal raids on London. The first of these was on 7 September and began what became known as 'the Blitz' – the heavy German air-raids over Britain's cities. This lasted until May 1941.

At first, London was the only target. It was bombed for 76 nights in a row from 7 September. But in November the Germans added Coventry and other cities, such as Liverpool, Plymouth and Birmingham, to their list of targets. Coventry was a particular target because of the aircraft factories there.

A On 13 September 1940 some German bombs fell on Buckingham Palace. The bombs damaged some outer buildings. King George VI and Queen Elizabeth were both pleased that the Palace had been hit because, as the Queen said, 'It makes me feel I can look the East End [of London] in the face.' Churchill was quick to see the propaganda value of the raid – unlike the Ministry of Information which had censored the news. He ordered the attack to be given maximum publicity. Can you suggest why?

At first there was little London's air defences could do against the raids. Searchlights at this time were not effective at altitudes above 3600 metres and so the German bombers simply flew above this height. RAF night fighters scored few successes. In one particularly heavy raid on 15 October the RAF managed to shoot down just one of the 400 bombers involved.

From February 1941 the Germans' main targets were the ports in the west of Britain. These were the main ports for supplies from the United States. Between February and May 1941 46 raids were made against ports such as Plymouth, Swansea, Belfast and Portsmouth, while London was bombed only seven times.

When anti-aircraft shells exploded they showered lethal shrapnel back down on the city, injuring civilians below.

The Home Guard

In May 1940 the government hurriedly set up the Local Defence Volunteers to deal with the possibility of a German invasion by parachutists. They were a second line of defence, consisting of men too young or too old to serve in the regular army. Their job was to patrol through the night to warn of any parachute landings. By June there were nearly 1.5 million of them.

Churchill suggested they change their names to the Home Guard but they still remained a figure of fun and were called 'Dad's Army'. At first, they had no guns or uniforms and paraded with broomsticks. They placed bed frames and old buses in fields to stop German gliders from landing. By 1942 the Home Guard was properly trained and equipped and numbered nearly two million.

The Baedeker raids

There were few raids after May 1941 until April 1942 when German planes bombed historic cities such as Exeter, York and Bath. These attacks were in revenge for RAF raids over German historic cities in March. One German spokesman described the attacks on these old English cities as 'Baedeker raids'. Baedeker was the name of a tourist guide to famous cities of cultural interest. The phrase was a propaganda disaster for the Germans because it implied they really were barbarians with no respect for culture.

The second Blitz

In the middle of 1944 Hitler launched the first of his secret 'Vengeance' weapons – the V-1. Hitler was determined to pay back the Allies for their 'terror' bombing of German cities. The V-1 was a rocket-powered flying bomb which had no pilot. After flying a fixed number of kilometres, the engine cut out and the rocket crashed to the ground.

The V-1 was difficult but not impossible to shoot down. The sound of its droning engine and then the terrible silence as it cut out brought terror to Londoners for the last nine months of the war. Just over 10 000 were launched against England but only 3500 of these found a target, killing 6200 people. The rest were shot down or crashed before reaching the coast.

B 3500 V-1 flying bombs fell on England. 2400 of these struck London. Londoners nicknamed them 'Doodlebugs'.

The next terror weapon was the V-2. It carried only a slightly bigger explosive load (1000 kilograms) than the V-1. But, unlike the V-1, the V-2 could not be stopped since it was a rocket which reached a speed of 4000 kilometres per hour before impact. It exploded without warning. From September 1944 until the end of March 1945 an average of five a day fell on England, killing nearly 3000 civilians. These were powerful weapons but it's worth pointing out that the RAF's Lancaster bombers were able to drop bombs with 5400 kilograms of explosives over Germany from June 1944.

What did the Blitz achieve?

The Blitz cost the Luftwaffe very few aircraft. In a raid by 200 aircraft the Germans would lose only three planes on average. German defences against the RAF were more effective and the British could expect to lose 15 planes for every 200 sent. The raids over Britain had no real effect on British aircraft production.

40 000 British civilians were killed and two million made homeless but it did not destroy the morale of the civilian population. Goebbels, Hitler's propaganda chief, decided that the British were showing such toughness because they were a 'Germanic race'.

President Roosevelt found it easier to persuade American opinion that now Britain was worth backing with vital military equipment and supplies. Strangely, the Blitz may have helped to improve morale since it did create a sense of community and shared danger which brought people closer together.

One lesson which the RAF's Bomber Command might have learned from the Blitz was that it was not easy to bomb a determined people into defeat. Air Chief Marshall Harris believed that RAF Bomber Command could do to the Germans what the Luftwaffe could not do to the British. He was wrong. But the bombing campaign over Germany did achieve other valuable results (see Chapter 11).

C They may have been dirty and smelly but London's underground stations made very popular shelters during the Blitz. Eventually some were equipped with bunk beds and toilets, and tickets were issued for regular users to reserve a bunk.

1 What was the 'Blitz'?
2 Why were ports particular targets for German bombers?
3 What lesson about the effect of bombing on morale should both Britain and Germany have learned?
4 'The V weapons were more frightening than destructive.' What is your opinion of this view?

HOW DID PEOPLE COPE?

Though Britain's anti-aircraft defences didn't have much success against German bombers, other measures were taken to make it difficult for the enemy. All street and shop lights were turned off and homes had their windows blacked out with thick curtains or blinds. The black-out was supposed to make it more difficult for German bombers to find their targets at night. A city like London with all its lights on would be easily found otherwise.

Taking shelter

By the time the war started 38 million gas masks had already been issued. These were never needed since gas was not used in the Second World War – although people weren't to know this at the time. For a long time civilians carried their gas masks about with them in case of a gas attack. Even babies' prams were made gas-proof.

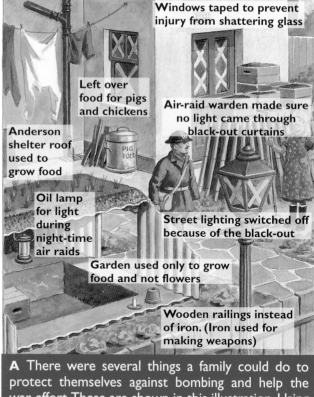

Windows taped to prevent injury from shattering glass

Left over food for pigs and chickens

Air-raid warden made sure no light came through black-out curtains

Anderson shelter roof used to grow food

Oil lamp for light during night-time air raids

Street lighting switched off because of the black-out

Garden used only to grow food and not flowers

Wooden railings instead of iron. (Iron used for making weapons)

A There were several things a family could do to protect themselves against bombing and help the war effort. These are shown in this illustration. Using your garden for flowers was considered unpatriotic – the 'Dig for Victory' campaign urged people to use all available space for growing vegetables. This patriotic householder has even used the top of the Anderson shelter for growing food.

The real danger, though, came not from gas but bombs and the government had already begun to prepare for air raids by issuing Anderson shelters as early as February 1939. Two million of these had been given to families in cities likely to be bombed by the time war broke out. They were free to families earning less than £250 a year. This was at a time when the average worker's wage was about £300 a year. Made from curved corrugated steel sheets bolted together, they were half buried in the garden. They were not very popular because they were damp and tended to flood. But most people preferred them to the communal brick shelters the government provided for the people in the local area.

B The government tried hard to persuade people to use the communal brick-built shelters. Here the side wall of one shelter has been cut away to show the public how there is room for whole families in them. Despite this, they remained unpopular. Built only of brick, with flat roofs and at ground level, they seemed to offer no better protection than Anderson shelters.

What Londoners really wanted to use were the underground stations. At first the government would not allow them to be used as shelters. It was afraid that the people, once inside these deep shelters, wouldn't come out and this would be bad for morale. But in October 1940 the government had to give in and they were opened up.

The most popular stations were the deepest, such as Hampstead, and queues for these began as early as 10 am. In the deepest ones you couldn't hear the noise of the bombs and so had a better chance of getting some sleep. People were desperate for a place on the platform and fights occasionally took place.

After 10 pm the current was switched off and Londoners could sleep along the track. Those who couldn't get to the platform had to make do with a night on the stairs or escalators. At first there were no proper toilet facilities and the best that could be arranged were a few buckets screened off with a blanket.

'Meals on wheels'

In October 1940 a new Home Secretary, Herbert Morrison, was appointed. He immediately ordered deep shelters to be built for 70 000 people – though these weren't ready before the Blitz ended in May 1941. But 200 000 bunks and proper toilets were ready in the tube stations by Christmas 1940. Morrison also arranged for tube trains equipped with food and drink to pass each evening and early morning through those stations used as shelters.

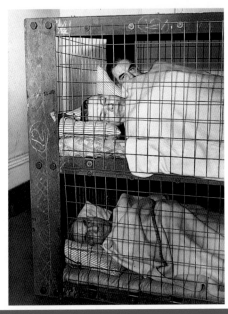

C A two-tiered Morrison shelter from the 1942 government catalogue – the ultimate in comfort and luxury. They were free to poorer families. They were designed to protect people from collapsing rubble and were used indoors – unlike the cold and damp Anderson shelters.

'Last orders'?

The tube stations were used by only about 15 per cent of the London population. More than half preferred to sleep in their own homes where they used steel-framed Morrison shelters inside the house. These were about the same height as a table and big enough for a couple of adults and children to shelter beneath. Most of the rest used their Anderson shelters or the public shelters. Some, though, used no shelters at all and simply sat out the raids in pubs, singing very loudly so as not to hear the sound of the bombs. In some cases, no doubt, 'last orders' meant exactly that. Those who lived in cities outside London had no tube stations in which to shelter. Many of these simply 'trekked' each night out into the country

and slept where they could – barns, cowsheds, even ditches. There were 50 000 trekkers each night out of Plymouth. The government disapproved of trekking because it suggested that morale was cracking.

Cleaning up

The government had expected air raids and the devastation they would bring. What the government was not ready for were the large numbers of *survivors*. Help for those who had lost their homes was very badly organised at first. Eventually compensation was paid for loss of homes and property. The houses of those who had left the cities were taken over and used to house the homeless.

Theft from bomb-damaged houses and shops (looting) could lead to the death penalty but this drastic measure was never used. However, looting did go on. It was not unusual for rescue workers, firemen or demolition workers to help themselves to the odd possession left in a bombed-out house. It was seen, almost, as a reward for the gruesome and dangerous job they had.

1 What was the idea behind the black-out?
2 Why were the deepest underground stations the most popular shelters?
3 Do you think the government should have distributed shelters free to all homes rather than make some people pay?
4 What do you think were the advantages and disadvantages of each of the following types of shelter? Which one would you have preferred to use?
   a) Morrison shelter;
   b) Anderson shelter;
   c) ground-level brick shelters;
   d) underground stations.

THE EFFECTS OF BOMBING AND MORALE

Not all the bombs dropped by the Germans were supposed to explode when they hit the ground. Some, called parachute mines, came down slowly attached to parachutes, and exploded above or on the ground. These could cause more damage than the usual iron-cased bombs which sometimes buried themselves deep into the ground before exploding. This reduced the impact of the explosion.

Others were delayed-action bombs and were timed to explode hours and even days after they had hit the ground. These were very irritating and caused more disruption than ordinary impact bombs. This was because everyone within 600 metres of such a bomb had to be moved until it had been defused or went off.

None of the shelters protected you from a direct hit or from the blast of a near miss. Victims of blast often showed no signs of injury. The blast pressure simply crushed the internal organs of the body and sometimes stripped the clothes off them. Sometimes the blast would tear bodies apart. Recovering the pieces, as source A describes, was not a pleasant job.

A Harry Meachun was an auxiliary policeman. He was called to a factory which had been hit:

I counted nine bodies along one of the benches with no visible signs at all upon them … It was blast that caused it, it had blown all their clothes off, including their boots and socks. They were just naked and dead … I think I picked up four heads that people were walking over … I remember bringing out one fellow. He'd lost half his face and down one side his arm was gone and his leg was gone and he looked up at me … and he said: 'Will you tell my landlady that I shall not be home to tea?' And with that he closed his eyes and was gone.

Rescue work

Rescue work was a difficult job. Workers were paid about £3 a week – much less than the average wage at the time. Former building workers made the best rescue workers because they had a good knowledge of how the buildings had been made and where to look for survivors. The risk from collapsing buildings and broken water and gas pipes all made rescue work more difficult and dangerous. Some 5000 building workers had to be released from the army to help with the repairs to bomb-damaged homes. Accommodation for those who lost their homes was very poor to begin with. For instance, 200–300 people crammed into a hall with only ten buckets for toilets was not unusual. Eventually, the government provided temporary housing like the one shown in source B.

B Temporary accommodation in Teddington, Middlesex, 1940. People whose homes had been bombed would be grateful for this sort of accommodation. Most had to make do with camp beds in smelly halls but the government preferred this image of the homeless family in 1940.

Did morale hold up?

What the government feared most was defeatism among the population. Defeatism was the idea that the war couldn't be won and that Britain should agree peace terms with the Germans. Mass Observation reported very few examples of defeatist views but there was evidence of racial prejudice and a need to have someone innocent to blame. There were complaints, for example, against Jews for 'grabbing the best shelters' or 'not helping with the war effort'. One woman remembered her wartime schooldays and how a Jewish pupil was 'terribly, terribly victimised' and 'the terrible attitude that the Jews almost got what they deserved'.

Looting was another sign of morale under strain, as were the occasions when Churchill and the King and Queen were booed when they visited bombed streets in the East End. There was also bad feeling between the upper and lower classes. Plush West End hotels had their own *private* and comfortable shelters which the ordinary population couldn't use. On one occasion this led to protesters occupying the shelter of the Savoy hotel.

This ill-feeling was made worse by the fact that most German bombs fell on the working class, industrial areas of big cities such as the East End of London. Few fell on the richer West End or comfortable suburbs. It seemed to some, therefore, that the poor were doing more than their fair share for the war.

C A family of Londoners with what's left of their Anderson shelter. This clearly posed photograph shows them with the cheery 'thumbs up' gesture. Posed or not, there is plenty of evidence to suggest that Britain's civilian population did show just this sort of rugged spirit.

Despite all this, morale *did* hold up and the civilian population remained firmly behind Churchill's policy of continuing the war until it was won. A different kind of spirit gradually emerged. As the historian, Peter Lewis, put it, 'Londoners as a whole did not lose their nerve, but they lost their reserve.'

D The Ministry of Home Security reported this situation in Portsmouth during the Blitz:

On all sides we hear that looting had reached an alarming level. The police seem unable to keep control … This seems another example of the lack of community spirit. The effect on morale is bad and there is a general feeling of desperation as there seems to be no solution.

E Harold Nicolson, a minister in the Ministry of Information, wrote this in his diary for 17 September, 1940:

Everybody is worried about the feeling in the East End, where there is much bitterness. It is said that even the King and Queen were booed the other day when they visited the destroyed areas. Clem [Atlee, the leader of the Labour Party] says that if only the Germans had the sense not to bomb west of London Bridge there might be a revolution in this country.

F Invasion imminent! If the Germans did invade it was hoped that removing road signs might at least confuse them. Fortunately, thanks to the Battle of Britain, the Germans never came and the only people confused by this were English visitors.

Q

1 Why did parachute mines cause more damage than ordinary bombs?
2 a) What do you think was the worst part of being involved in rescue work?
  b) Why do you think people still volunteered to do it?
3 Explain why i) source D and ii) source E would have been especially worrying for the government?
4 Why should a historian consider both sources D and E as valuable evidence about the effects of the Blitz? (Think about the provenance of these sources – especially the authors.)
5 'The morale of Britain's civilian population was on the point of breaking when the Blitz ended in May 1941.' Using the sources and the information in the text, explain whether you agree or disagree with this interpretation.

Evacuation

What was it like to be evacuated? What effects did it have?

Evacuation involved moving all of Britain's children from cities likely to be bombed to safer areas in the country. Plans already existed to evacuate Britain's children and they were quickly put into action in September 1939. 800 000 schoolchildren and 520 000 children under five (with their mothers) were soon sent by train to the country areas of Britain.

Evacuation was not compulsory and not all parents could bear to let their children go to stay with people they didn't know. This reluctance was understandable. But parents also knew that big

cities were likely targets for German bombing. During the period of the 'phoney war' (September 1939 – April 1940) there were no air raids. Gradually the parents arranged for their children to come back – only to go through it all again in September 1940 (and a third time during the V-bomb raids of 1944).

The problems

People with a spare room in country areas had to take in one or more children. The only choice they had was over which child they could take. Teachers went with their pupils too. They would all be crammed into the nearest available school and shared classrooms. When the evacuated children, or evacuees as they were called, arrived they were lined up for the host families to inspect. Clean looking girls were the most popular – they could help with domestic chores. Boys, though, were valued if they were big enough to help on the farm.

Sometimes brothers and sisters were split up, and dirty or unattractive children were left to last. All this proved to be a frightening experience for children a long way from their parents. Hosts were given an allowance of ten shillings (50p) a week – not much when a pair of stockings cost five shillings (25p). Some, nonetheless, tried to make money by providing very little for the children staying with them.

Some children didn't know how to use a toilet properly. In some inner city slums lacking proper toilets it was common practice to urinate on newspaper. Of course, their new, often middle-class hosts were horrified by such behaviour. The children often arrived with skin diseases and lice, and had never worn underwear, taken a bath or brushed their teeth. Bed-wetting, bad language and theft were other frequent complaints.

> One child explained his stealing because 'I've got to practise. My dad's a burglar and I'm going to be one when I grow up.'

'I wear underpants, do you?'

For children like these from inner city slums, life in the country was another world. Green fields, orchards and farm animals were all new to them. One wrote to his mother, 'They call this spring,

A By January 1940 most parents had arranged for their children to be brought back. The government tried hard to persuade them to leave the children where they were with posters like this one. The campaign, not surprisingly, was not a great success.

Mum, and they have one down here every year'. One delighted boy from the East End of London boasted to his friends: 'I wear underpants, do you?'

Many children loved the years they spent as evacuees as they enjoyed the benefits of country life: a healthy diet, fresh air and endless adventure. These children sometimes found it very difficult to get used to their old way of life when they returned to their homes after their evacuation.

Not all children, though, were sent to comfortable homes in delightful countryside. Some

B Happy, excited children on their way to their new home in the country. This was the official image the government was keen to encourage. The child on the left, though, doesn't seem quite so enthusiastic. The teacher on the left also seems to have her name and address label tied to her coat in case she forgets them!

found themselves in much the same conditions they had left behind and others were worse off. Children's experiences of evacuation, therefore, were very different. But for all of them there was homesickness and the worry that their parents might be killed in an air raid. The government did provide cheap train tickets for parents to visit their children but only once a month.

Consequences of evacuation

The evacuation of so many children had very important social and political effects. Country families were often shocked by the health of the children they took in and the poverty they lived in when at home. It helped to convince people that a

basic minimum standard of health and housing was a right for everyone. This was accepted during the war and the 1942 Beveridge Report promised changes (see Chapter 27). This set up what became known as the Welfare State in the years after the war.

In this sense, therefore, evacuation helped to bring about an important change in social attitudes. This in turn helped to bring about a new political belief that the state had a duty to provide much more in the way of basic standards of health and housing.

C Some evacuees were astonished by their new home, as this 13-year-old later wrote:

Everything was so clean in our room. We were given flannels and toothbrushes. We'd never cleaned our teeth until then. Hot water came from the tap … and there was a lavatory upstairs … this was all rather odd and rather scaring.

D The eyes of many country people were opened to the lives children led in their city slums. One woman remembered the four East End of London children sent to her:

… how tragic those children were. They couldn't get used to the open space and the quietness, particularly at night. They also couldn't understand why I never went to the pub. When their family came to see them, carrying a baby, they spent a little while with the children, then dumped the baby with me and departed to the local pub until closing time. The children didn't seem to mind. It must have been what they were used to.

Q

1. What did evacuation involve?
2. Why was the decision whether to evacuate their children such a difficult one for parents?
3. How does source A try to persuade parents not to bring their children back home?
4. What does source D suggest about the way some parents brought up their children?
5. a) Why do you think the government was keen to use photographs like the one in source B?
   b) How useful do you think this source is as evidence about the evacuation of children?
6. The poster in source A wasn't very successful in stopping parents bringing their children back. Your task is to design a better one.

Food Supplies and Rationing

Rationing in the First World War started in the last year of the war. This time, the government was much quicker to ration food and essential supplies. On the whole, the population approved of rationing as a way to make sure everyone got a fair share of what was available at a reasonable price. Without rationing and price control, prices would have shot up beyond the ability of ordinary people to pay.

Prices of rationed goods were controlled but if the price was set too low the supply simply dried up. This happened to tomatoes when the government cut their price in the pound by half. On the other hand, if the price was not controlled items in short supply cost a small fortune. A bunch of grapes, at £1 a bunch, could cost four times the price of a restaurant meal.

In November 1941 the government copied the system used by the Germans: giving each rationed item a points score. Items which were in shortest supply cost the most points. For example, half a kilogram of tinned salmon would use up 32 points but a tin of tomatoes would cost six points. Each month a person had 20 points to 'spend' on such goods.

Alternatives to the usual items were also found. Tea made from nettles was not popular but it had the edge over acorn coffee. Even less popular were dried eggs. Real eggs were very hard to come by. Egg powder, imported from the United States, was mixed with water and tasted like chalk. Another new food imported from the United

B Silk stockings were very hard to get hold of during the war and very expensive. A cheaper alternative was to have stockings painted on with gravy browning for the equivalent of only 35 pence a leg in today's money.

States was 'Spam' (Supply Pressed American Meat). In 1944 the weekly cheese allowance per person dropped to under 60 grams – roughly a block of 4 centimetres by 7 centimetres.

People could not buy rationed goods where they wanted. They had to use the shopkeeper

> **Paper was rationed. People had to use newspaper for toilet paper.**

where they were registered. The amount of supplies a shopkeeper got depended on the number of customers registered with him. When customers 'bought' goods he stamped the customers' ration cards and deducted the number of points used up. Sweets were also rationed. The monthly allowance was 250 grams of chocolate or its equivalent. But children's teeth were far healthier as a result.

Beating the system

One way to save on food coupons was to eat out. The fact that the rich could eat fine meals in splendid hotels and get round the problem of rationing caused some anger in the working-class

A This is a list of rationed goods and dates of rationing. Eggs and milk were also rationed but bread, potatoes, and fresh vegetables, fruit and fish were not.

Petrol	September	1939
Butter, bacon and sugar	January	1940
Meat	March	1940
Tea and margarine	July	1940
Sale of silk stockings banned	December	1940
Cosmetics (except lipstick)	February	1941
Clothes	June	1941
Points system for rationing introduced	November	1941

areas. The government decided that this was unfair. From 1942 restaurants (apart from the six plushest London hotels) were not allowed to charge more than five shillings (25p) for a meal – about three times the price of a packet of 20 cigarettes.

In 1943 the government set up 'British restaurants' which charged only one shilling (5p) for a very basic meal. This ready supply of cheap and nutritious food helped to make sure that the diet of the British population was much better during the war than it had ever been before.

Another way to get round rationing was to buy items on the black market. This was illegal but common, and items were expensive. Officials at the docks could be bribed to allow a few 'extra' items to be loaded onto a truck. These would then be delivered to the butcher's or greengrocer's shop. Shopkeepers would sell these from 'under

the counter' to their best (and most trusted) customers. Customers went out of their way to be pleasant to their shopkeepers, especially butchers.

A more patriotic way to get round rationing was to grow your own food. The 'Dig for Victory' campaign encouraged people to grow their own vegetables in gardens and allotments. In 1939 there were 815 000 allotments but these had increased to 1.4 million in 1943.

Utility

In 1942 the government introduced the Utility symbol. Goods with this symbol were made cheaply but to a good standard. Clothing and furniture became Utility products and could be bought with coupons. These were sometimes half the price of non-utility items but the styles were very basic. Men's trousers were made without turn-ups. This was very unpopular. Women were encouraged to wear Utility suits (a one-piece trouser suit with a zip or buttons). These suits were especially recommended for use in shelters.

At least these suits meant that women didn't have to spend time hunting down pairs of stockings or painting their legs with gravy browning (see sources B and D).

·· every available piece of land must be cultivated

GROW YOUR OWN FOOD
supply your own cookhouse

C As food became more and more difficult to import, the government did its best to encourage the population to grow their own. Rationing made this an even more attractive option.

D Gravy browning, though a cheap solution when stockings were in short supply and very expensive, had its problems as one 18-year-old recalls:

We used to put this gravy browning all over our legs and your friend would stand at the back with a black pen or eyebrow pencil and she'd mark a seam down the back. Mind you, if it rained you were in a right mess. The dogs used to come round, sniffing your legs.

1 Why were most people in favour of rationing?
2 Why did it pay for people to be nice to their local shopkeepers?
3 Why do you think the people's diet was such a healthy one during the war? Think about the types of food in short supply and those which were not rationed.
4 How do you think the 'Dig for Victory' campaign helped towards the war effort?
5 a) How did the government try to stop ill-feeling between the rich and poor?
   b) Do you think it did enough?

Women in the Workforce

'This war is everybody's'

In November 1939 the editor of the magazine *Mother and Home* wrote: 'The last was a soldier's war. This one is everybody's.' The purpose of this and the next two chapters is to decide just how much the war did change things for women.

Certainly, the statistics suggest that a lot did change. By September 1943 there were nearly eight million women in paid work. This is three million more than when the war started. There were another one million women in the Women's Voluntary Services. The munitions industries saw a big increase in women workers – up from 500 000 to two million. From December 1941 women between the ages of 20 and 30 could be conscripted into the women's armed forces – though not for combat duty.

In the same year women between 18 and 40 could be made to work in war industries. In 1943 the government widened these age limits so more women could be used. By then nine out of every ten single women were doing some kind of war work.

'Nice girls don't'

After 1941 the government could tell single women to go to any part of the country and to work in whatever industry it decided. It could also order them to join one of the women's armed services (see Chapter 22). The government had asked women to volunteer for a variety of war industries but the response hadn't been good. Women were afraid that they would be sent away from home and forced to stay with strangers (called 'being **billeted**'). Factory work with its 12-hour shifts was not appealing to women, and fathers and boyfriends tended to object to them working as well. There still remained an attitude that 'nice girls' didn't work in factories.

Dilution

The government, at first, didn't conscript married women, and women with children under 14 couldn't be sent to work away from home. But from 1943 the government began finding work for married women as well. It must be said that the

JUST A GOOD AFTERNOON'S WORK

A Government propaganda encouraging women to do factory work had limited success. This poster at least had a touch of humour on its side.

attitudes of male workers, in some cases, were not welcoming. They were afraid that unskilled women would start doing skilled, male workers' jobs and for less money. This was known as dilution. Dilution, they argued, would force down wages and cost skilled workers their jobs.

These men's fears were increased when women were promised equal pay for doing the same job as men. However, this was easily got round. The job done by women – even if identical to that done by men – was simply renamed and paid a lower rate. The government didn't help the cause of women's equality, either. It refused to pay its women civilian and military employees the same rate as men.

> Churchill threatened to resign in 1944 if women teachers were paid the same as men.

The difference in rates of pay angered most women. In some cases, they weren't even paid the men's *unskilled* rate for the skilled work they were doing.

B Kay Ekevall represented women workers in the shipbuilding firm, Redpath Brown. She remembers what it was like working alongside men:

Women took part in most of the jobs, such as crane-driving, painting, welding. I became a welder when there were both men and women trainees, but the men were paid more than the women. We had several battles over equal pay after we were used on the same jobs as the men … By the end of my time we had managed to get close to the men's wage. On the whole the men didn't seem to resent the women, and the skilled men were friendly and helpful to the trainees. As it was an essential war industry … I suppose they weren't afraid for their jobs. I believe there was some resentment in other factories at the dilution by cheap labour.

The government failed in other areas, too. Only one child in four under the age of five was in a public nursery. The mothers of the other children had to make their own arrangements for child care while they worked. Even when concessions were made, there was a sting in the tail. A 12-hour shift meant that the shops were closed when the women finished work. The only thing they could do, therefore, was to miss work if they needed to go shopping.

This explains why absenteeism among women was twice the rate it was for men. Women working a full week of 57–60 hours were given 'shopping time' to allow them to get essential shopping done in working hours. Shopping for supplies in wartime Britain was a difficult task and many women must have felt their working day never ended.

C Not all women, it seems, wanted equal pay. This is what one woman told Mass Observation in 1942:

I do feel that equal pay would upset the relations between the sexes. Personally, I like a man to have more money than me. It gives me twice as much pleasure to have a dress bought for me by a kindly man than to buy it myself, and this is because I am feminine.

Despite all this, many women were pleased to be involved in useful work which helped the war effort. Even if they weren't as well paid as the men, they were still earning much more than they were used to getting before the war. Before the war women earned in the region of £2 a week and men about £3. During the war some women doing dangerous munitions work were earning £10 a week and £5 was common in the aircraft industry.

D This woman is at work in a munitions factory and is manufacturing a bomb for an aircraft. This work was both skilled and dangerous and explains why some women like her could earn as much as £10 a week. This was five times the average female wage before the war.

1 What evidence is there that more women found jobs because of the war?
2 There were several reasons why women weren't keen on factory work. What were they and which one do you think was most important in discouraging them? Explain your answer.
3 Explain what you think Kay Ekevall in source B meant by:
   a) 'As it was an essential war industry … I suppose they weren't afraid for their jobs.'
   b) 'I believe there was some resentment in other factories at the dilution by cheap labour.'
4 a) What are the differences in attitude to equal pay for women in sources B and C?
   b) Why is source C less useful to a historian who wants to know how typical these views were?
5 It may be that the view of the woman in source C is heard less often nowadays. Do you think it was more common then? Give a reason for your answer.
6 'The government didn't do as much as it should have done to help women workers during the war.' Explain whether you agree or disagree with this view.

22

Women in the Armed Forces

Key Issues	**What was life in the services like for women? Were their fears justified? Were sexist attitudes a problem?**

When women were conscripted in 1941 they were, in theory, given the choice of joining one of the armed forces or working in the factories. They could join either the Women's Royal Naval Service known as Wrens (WRNS), the Women's Auxiliary Air Force (WAAF), or the Auxiliary Territorial Service (ATS).

The WRNS was the most popular service, followed by the WAAF. For one thing women thought their blue uniforms were more attractive and feminine than the dull khaki of the ATS. The writer of one letter to *The Times* in 1941 complained that: 'Khaki is a colour detested by every woman and makes a well-developed girl look vulgar.'

In practice, women who were conscripted had no choice as to which of the services they joined. The WRNS and WAAF already had waiting lists so all the new conscripts had to join the ATS. In 1944 there were 450 000 women in these three services with

212 000 of them in the ATS. This allowed many men to do combat duty and this was an important part of women's contribution to the war effort.

Women in the WRNS and the WAAF were generally thought to be more respectable while those in the army's ATS had a 'reputation' for loose behaviour. Such ideas about women in uniform did not make it easy for women to join and many were not keen. Public opinion could be very hurtful, and husbands and fathers were even more against their womenfolk joining one of the armed forces than they were against them working.

The general belief was that single women in the armed services were more likely to get pregnant than single women in civilian jobs. Government statistics proved the opposite was true but the old attitudes lived on.

'Toilets with doors, please!'

Women's fears about life in the armed services were probably made worse by finding out that the lavatories had no doors on them. This was common practice for the men and nobody had given much thought to the idea that women would be unhappy with the arrangement.

Women soon found themselves doing tough and dangerous jobs. They worked as mechanics, welders, pilots, carpenters and gunners on anti-aircraft guns – though they weren't allowed to fire the guns. They also operated the searchlights for the anti-aircraft guns. The ATS was certainly the most dangerous of the services open to women. 335 were killed and another 300 wounded. Women also served as ferry pilots, flying the newly built planes to their air bases.

But it should be remembered that traditional, sexist attitudes did not suddenly disappear. The vast majority of women in these services worked as cleaners, cooks and secretaries. Women ferry pilots flew planes without radios because RAF chiefs feared they would use them to gossip to each other! This type of flying, called instrument-flying, was more difficult and sometimes caused problems as source C proves.

Some women so hated the ATS that they deliberately got pregnant to get themselves dismissed from the army.

A Most ATS women were used as cooks, typists and clerks. Some, though, found themselves doing what would have been considered men's jobs before the war. The original caption for this photograph says: 'these women are servicing six-ton trucks – an 'unglamorous job'.'

Full information
at the nearest recruiting centre
or your employment exchange

B This poster urging women to join the ATS or WAAF was issued in 1943. It suggests that the earlier recruitment attempts hadn't yet filled all the vacancies.

C One ferry pilot, Diana Barnato Walker, remembered this incident after coming off 'leave' – the military equivalent of being on holiday. She got lost in clouds before she had learned properly to instrument-fly and was very close to the ground and off course.

I'd just come off leave and was still wearing a skirt and stockings. I thought 'I can't bail out because I'll look so silly coming down with my stockings and panties showing'. It was so stupid. I should have bailed out. [She managed, though, to land on a flooded airfield] … I got out of the cockpit and my knees collapsed. I was so frightened. I couldn't let the ground crew know that, so I pretended to kneel down to get my bag out of the plane. When we went into the hut I stole a glance at the bulletin board to see where I was – I didn't want to ask.

The decision in 1941 to have mixed anti-aircraft gun units was a controversial one. Not even the fact that Churchill's daughter worked on one helped to get rid of ugly rumours about the women in these units (source D). There were about 50 000 women in the ATS who helped to operate anti-aircraft guns. The fact that they had to share accommodation with the men and lived close to each other led to heavy criticism.

D Joan Savage Cowey worked in a mixed anti-aircraft gun crew.

There was a feeling that we were sort of loose women living in tents with men. They called us 'officers' groundsheets' – we got that all the time. They thought we were there to entertain the troops. The American soldiers were worse. They'd say the Brits had it really good, having us girls along to keep them happy. The whole thing – all the criticism of us – just had to do with sex.

Women in the armed services had to operate under double standards. They were expected to do skilled, tough and sometimes dangerous jobs and yet still be feminine. This created extra strains for women which the men didn't have, as Diana Barnato Walker points out in source E.

E Another extract from Diana Barnato Walker's experiences as a ferry pilot:

I always thought, if I crashed, I'd rather be killed than disabled. A damaged woman has nothing. Men can function without a leg or arm, or burnt, and they are considered heroes. People accept them. But a damaged woman? I think it was my greatest fear.

1 Why was the ATS less popular than the other women's services?
2 The poster in source B invites women to join either the ATS or the WAAF. Why might the government be accused of misleading women in the choice offered?
3 What evidence is there in the text that sexist attitudes were still strong during the war?
4 Why do you think the woman pilot in source C didn't want to ask what airfield she'd landed on?
5 Do you agree with the point Diana Barnato Walker makes in source E? Explain your answer.

23

'The Friendly Invasion' – GIs and British Women

Did the presence of American GIs affect the morale of British servicemen? Were the strains on family life already in evidence?

The war affected how women behaved in many ways. For one thing, they had to cope with raising their children without the help of their husbands. They had to do this and do war work or enlist in the armed forces, too. Acts of petty crime by children increased and the existence of so many families without fathers was blamed.

Crime in general increased by nearly 50 per cent during the war. No doubt criminals were helped by the fact that the number of policemen fell by a quarter to 43 000. The opportunity for having affairs added greatly to the problems of trying to keep marriages together. The presence of so many Americans didn't make this any easier.

The Yanks are coming

By June 1944 there were more than 1.5 million American servicemen, or GIs as they were called, in Britain. While women generally found them fascinating, British servicemen generally found them irritating and boastful. 'Over paid, over sexed, and over here' was one common view of American GIs.

The fact that they had smarter uniforms and were much better paid made

American troops were called GIs because all their equipment was given to them as 'General Issue'.

matters worse. An American private earned more than seven times what a British private earned and there wasn't much to spend it on – apart from British women. Americans had no trouble providing wonderful gifts of hard-to-get items, such as chocolate and stockings.

Lord Haw-Haw's broadcasts played on the concerns of British troops overseas. He told them that their wives and girlfriends were having affairs with these Americans while they were doing the fighting. British servicemen on leave in Britain often came to blows with Americans, especially in

pubs, and women were usually the reason. Reports of these incidents were **censored**. American troops were given advice by their own government on how to behave towards Britons (source A).

A Part of the American government's advice to their own servicemen:

> The British dislike bragging and showing off … The British serviceman can be very touchy about the difference in his wages and yours … Three actions on your part will slow up friendship – swiping his girl, not appreciating what his army has been up against and rubbing it in that you are better paid than he is.

Many British women did find GIs attractive. No doubt, Americans were responsible for a fair number of the 1.8 million illegitimate babies born during the war.

B American servicemen at their club, the Rainbow Corner in London, in 1945. Relations between British and American troops in Britain were tense. Fights took place – and news of these was kept quiet by the censors.

Black GIs

The United States army during the war was still a segregated one. Black troops and white troops were kept in separate units. They had separate facilities inside their camps and were told to use different bars and pubs outside them. They weren't even allowed to receive blood from a donor of a different colour. Many Britons found this attitude strange and they also found black GIs to be much better mannered than white ones (source C).

What British people didn't always realise was that American blacks had found that treating whites with exaggerated courtesy was the best way to survive in the United States. Churchill wasn't willing to upset the Americans over their treatment of black troops or even, it seems, over their treatment of blacks from the British colonies. A black official from one of Britain's colonies was turned away from his usual restaurant because some white American officers complained about him eating with them. Churchill took no action over the matter.

The strains on marriages

Many marriages broke up under the strain of separation. In 1939 only one marriage in every 100 ended in divorce. By 1945 it had gone up to five in every 100. Adultery (having sex with someone who isn't your marriage partner) was a big cause of divorce. The last 12 months of the war saw eight times as many husbands sue their wives for divorce because of adultery. Sometimes a marriage would fail for less obvious reasons than husbands or wives taking lovers. Men and women were changed by their experience of war and became different people (source E).

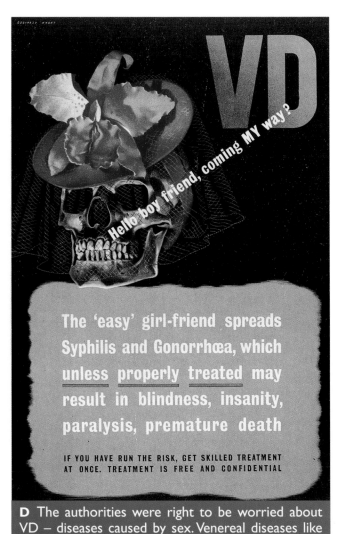

The 'easy' girl-friend spreads Syphilis and Gonorrhœa, which unless properly treated may result in blindness, insanity, paralysis, premature death

IF YOU HAVE RUN THE RISK, GET SKILLED TREATMENT AT ONCE. TREATMENT IS FREE AND CONFIDENTIAL

D The authorities were right to be worried about VD – diseases caused by sex. Venereal diseases like syphilis and gonorrhoea sometimes put more troops in hospital than the enemy. But the men were not easily discouraged – even by posters such as these.

E One woman remembered how difficult it was to adjust to married life again after the war:

When my husband came home we discovered we were two different people, so much had happened in those years apart. My husband came back … with the attitude of a sergeant-major. I am sure he expected me to jump up and salute when he entered a room … He was finding it hard to get a civilian job and having to take orders … I missed going to work and the companionship and intelligent conversation … There were times when I thought that if there was a hell on earth, I was living it. I did not want a divorce, I could never have left the children.

1 Why did British troops dislike American GIs so much?
2 Why do you think some British women liked them so much?
3 Why do you think that the government censored news of fights between British and American servicemen?
4 What evidence is there that the British government was not willing to upset the United States over the issue of racism?
5 Why do you think the war led to an increase in the number of divorces?

24

How Far Did the Role of Women Really Change?

Did women really find a new freedom during the war years? How far did men's attitudes change?

Women's Land Army

Attitudes to women working in farming saw dramatic changes. There was a desperate need for farm labour from the start of the war. Before September 1939 there had been 550 000 men working on the land and 55 000 women. The number of men dropped and 80 000 women joined the Women's Land Army (WLA) to make up the difference.

Farmers doubted that women could do the physically demanding and dirty work needed on Britain's farms. The idea that women could drive tractors, plough, cut down trees and shear sheep seemed daft. What made it more unlikely was that a third of the women came from the towns and were not used to country life at all. Women in the WLA had no choice where they worked. They were billeted in remote areas in very basic conditions. Many spoke of having to travel to the public baths for a proper wash.

WLA pay was poor. In 1944 they earned £2.40 a week – less than the female average wage of £3 – and half of that went on lodgings. Despite this, the Land Girls were a success. They proved themselves more than able to cope with the tough jobs and handled farm animals particularly well. Like women in the armed services, they had to put up with the same sexist comments about their supposed 'lack of moral standards'.

What did the war change for women?

Clearly the many varied, difficult and skilled jobs women did during the war proved that women could do nearly every job that men could do. Though they weren't expected to carry the same weights as men, they did the same jobs.

However, there is plenty of evidence to suggest that women never got away from their traditional role as far as people's thinking went. Men were not enthusiastic supporters of this new, independent role for women – and neither were many women. By June 1943 there were nearly eight million women in paid work but this had dropped to six million by June 1947.

This fall was not because the government tried hard to get women out of their wartime jobs to make room for men. There was a labour shortage after the war and the government was keen for women to stay in their jobs. They left their jobs because they wanted to return to the home. Government surveys in 1943 and again in 1947 revealed that 58 per cent of women believed that married women should not go out to work.

Many had delayed having children during the war and now they decided to start their families. However, some of these married women went on to find jobs in the 1950s. Source B suggests that it was more acceptable for married women, once they stopped having children, to work now than it was before the war.

A The government was keen to show this image of life as a member of the Women's Land Army. Three women tuck into lunch on a haystack. Forgotten are the 5 am starts in the freezing cold and the endless shovelling of muck.

B Percentage of women in paid work:			
	Single women	*Married women*	*All women*
1911	69	10	35
1921	68	9	34
1931	72	10	34
1951	73	22	35

ON SALE THURSDAY, SEPTEMBER 1st, 1949

WOMAN'S OWN
The National Women's Weekly

JUST MARRIED?
Our new homemaking series on page 26 is for YOU

C Any hopes that women had carved out a new role for themselves as a result of the war soon faded. This *Woman's Own* cover from 1949 suggests that, even though women now made better mixed doubles partners in tennis matches, their real role still remained 'homemaking'.

Women's career opportunities weren't drastically improved by the war, either. Women during the war found many jobs in new areas of employment such as metal manufacturing and engineering. But these opportunities only lasted as long as the war. The shutting down of nurseries after the war meant the end of jobs for women with children. They continued to make only slow progress in professions like medicine and law. By 1961 only 15 per cent of doctors and a mere 3.5 per cent of lawyers were women.

Equal pay?

After growing protests by women, the government agreed in 1944 to set up a Royal Commission to investigate the issue of equal pay for women. Conveniently, it didn't report until a year after the war in 1946. The average male manual worker's wage in 1943 was £5.70 a week while the wage for a woman was £3.

The Commission accepted this was true but reported that it was a difficult matter to judge because women often did different jobs from men and so equal pay wasn't an issue.

Respect

What could not be taken away from women was the new self-respect that the war had given them. There is no doubt that they were much more confident about themselves and their abilities. Many enjoyed the independence and freedom the war had given them. If these changes had come

too late for these women then their daughters would benefit in the late 1960s when the feminist movement began its campaign for women's rights.

D Mona Marshall worked in the steel industry during the war. She was in no doubt about what the war did for her:

To be quite honest, the war was the best thing that ever happened to us. I was as green as grass and terrified if anyone spoke to me. I had been brought up not to argue. My generation [of women] had been taught to do as we were told. At work you did exactly as your boss told you and you went home to do exactly as your husband told you. The war changed all that. The war made me stand on my own two feet.

E Pat Parker worked in the Women's Land Army. This is her opinion on those three and a half years:

[Those years were] absolutely fantastic. They were complete freedom, where I'd never known it before. I'd always had my father standing on the corner of the street saying, 'You should be indoors'. This was nine o'clock at night … And that went on until I was sixteen. Whereas being away, I could do what I liked. All of a sudden nobody was bothering me, my life was my own. It was really a marvellous time.

1 Why were there fewer women in work after the war?
2 According to source B what effect did the First and Second World Wars have on the overall employment of women?
3 Does source B suggest that the Second World War brought no real change for any of the three categories of women? Explain your answer.
4 How do the women in sources D and E agree about the way women benefited from the war?
5 In what ways does source C suggest a different image for women compared with source D?

Extended writing
'The Second World War brought no lasting changes for women.' Using the information and sources in Chapters 21–24, explain whether you agree or disagree with this interpretation. Remember to comment on social attitudes to women, employment prospects for women and what women themselves thought.

25

How Did the War Affect the Workers?

Why did the government take control over people's lives during the war? Did the workers co-operate or did they resent the government's interference?

The Second World War had a tremendous impact on the economy and the working lives of the British people. Never before had a British government taken such complete control of the country. The longer the war went on and the more desperate Britain's position became, the more drastic the measures were.

Emergency Powers Act

In May 1940 the government extended the Emergency Powers Act (EPA) of 1939. It now had 'complete control over persons and property'. Ernest Bevin, the Minister of Labour, had the right to send any adult to work in any industry in any part of the country. He also had the right to decide what hours that person would work and what wages they would be paid.

A Bevin would stop at nothing to improve the working conditions of workers – provided, of course, they didn't want to go on strike. Here factory workers get their hands massaged and finger nails painted in a 'Bevin Bar' in a London department store. However, nice hands weren't enough to stop an average of 1600 strikes a year during the war.

By the end of 1940 key industries were still short of workers. The government realised that the EPA would need to include women. In March 1941 they were conscripted into the workforce. In the same month, the Essential Work Order (EWO) gave

There was no unemployment during the war.

Bevin the right to make any worker stay in what he considered an 'essential' industry. In other words, an essential industry worker needed Bevin's permission to leave his or her job.

On the other hand, the EWO now guaranteed nearly six million workers a job with decent pay and conditions. Employers would find it very difficult to lay off any of their workers as all dismissed workers had the right to appeal to a tribunal.

Strikes

Bevin, a Labour Party member and leader of Britain's biggest trade union, banned strikes. He set up tribunals to settle disputes between workers and their employers. The trade union leaders accepted these changes because Bevin was one of them, but strikes still took place. There were frequent strikes in the docks, shipbuilding, aircraft and mining industries.

Some workers were determined to make the most of the chance the war gave them to earn high wages. They remembered only too well the bitterness of long periods without work in the 1930s. They also remembered how badly their fathers had been treated after the First World War. The miners were especially bitter about their treatment during and after the failed General Strike of 1926. As one miner put it later: 'I was aware there was a war going on, but my enemy was in the workplace … The enemy was management'.

Bevin boys

Coal output fell by 15 per cent during the war and in December 1943 Bevin was forced to introduce what became known as 'Bevin boys'. One man in every ten between the ages of 18 and 25 was chosen by ballot to work as a miner instead of being conscripted into the armed forces. This was to make up for labour shortages in a mining industry where 13 per cent of miners were, on average, absent from work every day in 1944.

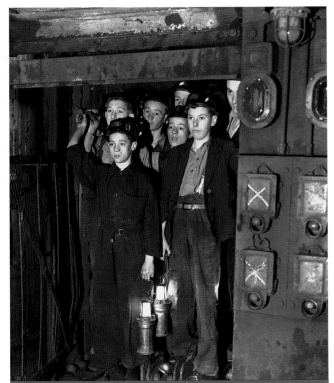

B 'Bevin boys' were forced to work in the mines and very few were thrilled by the prospect. Most wanted to serve in the armed forces. This group can't even raise a feeble, morale-boosting smile for the official photographer. About 7000 young men were sent to work in the mines as 'Bevin boys'.

Strikes by miners made up nearly half the days lost in strikes in most years of the war. The term 'days lost' measures strikes by multiplying each striking worker by the number of days he or she is on strike. So, 100 000 workers on strike for ten days gives one million 'days lost'. The most days lost in strikes took place in 1944 with 3.7 million days – compared to just 940 000 in 1940. The average for the war was two million days lost per year.

Though Bevin had the right to fine workers who went on strike, very few were fined and many of those who were fined didn't bother to pay. He realised that it was vital to keep the support of the workers. Harsh measures against striking workers might lose that support.

Miners were angry because they believed that women in war factories were earning much more than they were. Miners' wages were very low. They were eightieth in the wages table of 100 industries. The miners' union demanded a minimum of £6 a week but this was rejected. 220 000 miners in

South Wales and Yorkshire went on strike and got a better offer.

Generally, trade unions played a key role in helping the war effort, even though there were disputes in several industries. Public approval for unions can be measured by the increase in union membership during the war. In 1939 there were 6.2 million union members. This had increased to 8.2 million in 1943 – and two million of these were women. Bevin's own union, the Transport and General Workers' Union, was the first union to have one million members.

What happened to living standards?

Living standards for working-class people rose during the war. The average industrial earnings for men rose by 80 per cent while the cost of living for working-class men rose by just 50 per cent. Middle- and upper-class people didn't do so well. Their standard of living fell because their salaries didn't go up as much and they paid more in taxes than workers. Overall, the group which did best from the war were farmers. The group which did worst were the wives and children of ordinary servicemen. Their allowance from the government was low and they found it hard to borrow money because they were considered a 'bad risk'.

1 What did the Emergency Powers Act allow the government to do?
2 Why do you think the government thought it was necessary to introduce this policy?
3 Why were workers still willing to go on strike, even though their country was at war?
4 Do the figures for trade union membership during the war suggest that the trade unions were unpopular because of the strikes? Explain your answer.
5 Can you think of any reason why more workers were willing to go on strike in 1944 than they were in 1940? (Think about the military situation in each year.)
6 a) Why do you think the families of ordinary servicemen were thought to be 'bad risks' for borrowing money?
   b) Do you think this was fair?

26

How Good Was Churchill as a War Leader?

What made Churchill a good leader? Was he the sort of leader Britain needed during the war?

Winston Spencer Churchill had been in charge of the Royal Navy as First Lord of the Admiralty (1911–15) in the First World War. This was not a success for Churchill and he was forced to resign. Instead, he went to serve in the trenches as a 41-year-old infantry officer and this helped to establish his reputation as a fighter. He returned to a job in the government later in the war.

The Norwegian Campaign of April 1940 was Churchill's idea when he was, once again, First Lord of the Admiralty. The British force was badly equipped and its orders impossible to achieve. The entire plan was a disaster from the start. Churchill might have been forced to resign as he had to in 1915 over Gallipoli. But he was saved by the German invasion of western Europe on 10 May.

It was now clear that Britain needed a more aggressive leader than Chamberlain and Churchill was the obvious choice. Churchill gave the British a belief in themselves and he convinced them that the war would be won. This was something that Chamberlain could not do. Parliament voted for Churchill to be the new Prime Minister on 10 May.

Churchill's inspiring speeches were a major reason for his success. He was also willing now to forgive and forget quarrels with political opponents. His decision to appoint Bevin, a trade union leader, as Minister of Labour was a clever move. He knew that Bevin could win over trade union support – something that Churchill, a Conservative, could never have done.

Churchill and Roosevelt

Churchill knew that a British victory in the war depended on the USA becoming involved and he set out to achieve this. The Lend–Lease agreement of March 1941 drew the Americans closer to Britain. President Roosevelt promised to lend Britain vital war supplies and equipment on the understanding that their value would be repaid after the war. By the end of the war, the US had 'lent' $42 billion worth of equipment to Britain and the Soviet Union.

The relationship between Churchill and Roosevelt became very close. Roosevelt respected Churchill and recognised that he would fight to the end rather than surrender. This helped to convince Roosevelt that Britain was worth backing. Roosevelt justified American support for Britain by saying that if your neighbour's house was on fire, it would be stupid not to lend him your hose to put it out.

Churchill and Stalin

Churchill had always been a fierce opponent of communism and communist Russia. The German invasion of Russia in 1941 forced him to forget this hatred. Instead, Churchill welcomed communist Russia and its leader, Joseph Stalin, as Britain's ally in the war against Hitler. Churchill's relationship with Stalin was always tense – the two did not trust each other. Stalin suspected that Britain and the USA were both content to leave the fighting to Russia until Germany was almost beaten.

Roosevelt was more prepared to listen to Stalin's complaints. He partly shared Stalin's view that Churchill was looking for ways to weaken Russia's role in Europe after the war. Roosevelt more firmly agreed with Stalin's claim that Churchill was trying to keep the British Empire together at all costs. The United States had little sympathy with Churchill's efforts to save the British Empire.

There is evidence to suggest that Churchill did allow his *political* worries to influence *military* decisions. He frequently interfered in the plans of his generals. This could lead to mistakes and Churchill was ruthless enough to make others pay for them.

Churchill and his commanders

In 1941 Churchill was so desperate for a morale-boosting victory that he bullied General Wavell, the British commander of the forces in North Africa, into launching an attack before Wavell was ready. The attack failed and Churchill sacked Wavell. He then made Wavell's replacement, General Auchinleck, defend Tobruk when Auchinleck said the British should withdraw from the city. Tobruk was captured and 30 000 British troops were taken prisoner. Two months later in August 1942 Auchinleck was also replaced.

Churchill has also been criticised over his treatment of the commander of the RAF's Bomber Command, Air Chief Marshall Harris. Churchill encouraged Harris to bomb Germany's cities and even insisted on the controversial bombing of Dresden in February 1945. Harris didn't think Dresden was worth bombing because it had little industry but he carried out Churchill's orders. 50 000 civilians died in the raid. Six weeks later Churchill described it as 'an act of terror'. Harris took the blame for the raid but privately described Churchill's comment as an 'insult'.

DAKAR-MERS EL-KEBIR

A Vichy France had a different view of Churchill. Those French who worked with the Nazi occupiers showed Churchill as a laughing murderer. In July 1940, after France had surrendered, he ordered the Royal Navy to attack the French fleet at Mers El-Kebir to stop the Germans capturing it. 1300 French sailors were killed.

Was he a great wartime leader?

Clearly, Churchill made mistakes. He could be cruel and unfair towards those under him. After the failure of his Gallipoli campaign in 1915, Churchill got a reputation for supporting badly thought-out plans. This seems to have happened in the Second World War too. He also supported the use of the atomic bombs on Japan even though he knew the Japanese would surrender if they were allowed to keep their emperor.

But it was Churchill's fighting spirit in 1940 which picked British morale up off the floor. He refused to listen in 1940 to suggestions from his own ministers that Britain should consider a peace deal with Germany – despite the fact defeat seemed almost certain.

Churchill's skilful handling of Roosevelt gave Britain a powerful friend when the situation was desperate. In 1917, Churchill had said: 'There are only two ways of winning the war and they both begin with A.' Air power was one and America was the other. He believed the same in the Second World War. Roosevelt was only prepared to offer this support in the years before Pearl Harbor because he was convinced that Churchill meant to win the war.

What Churchill provided in the war years was exactly what Britain needed: determined, spirited leadership. He was a natural war leader. In the next chapter, though, we'll see that the British people decided they needed another kind of leader for the peace.

1 What does Churchill's decision to serve in the trenches in the First World War tell us about his character?
2 Why did Parliament prefer Churchill to Chamberlain as Prime Minister in May 1940?
3 Why was Hitler's invasion of western Europe in May 1940 a stroke of luck for Churchill personally?
4 'There are only two ways of winning the war and they both begin with A.' Do you think Churchill's comment was true for the Second World War? Give reasons for your answer.
5 Churchill has been criticised for two things:
   a) interfering with the plans of his commanders;
   b) treating his commanders unfairly.
   Provide evidence from the text for both of these criticisms. Which do you think is the most serious criticism and why?
6 The historian, Richard Lamb, has written this about Churchill: 'Despite many blunders and hasty … decisions, only one verdict is possible. He was a great wartime leader.' Using the evidence in this chapter, and any other material, explain whether you agree or disagree with this interpretation of Churchill.

27

How Did the War Change Britain?

How had the hopes of ordinary people been changed by the war? Why was Churchill so out of touch with the people?

Why did Churchill lose the 1945 election?

The war changed Britain a great deal and this became very obvious to Churchill as early as July 1945. He lost Britain's first general election for ten years. The reasons for Churchill's defeat sum up many of the changes which had taken place in six years of war.

Winston Churchill had been an inspiring leader of Britain. He became Prime Minister at a time when Britain seemed about to be invaded. After the defeat of France in June 1940, Britain faced the might of Hitler's military power alone. Defeat seemed likely. It was at this time that Churchill made his greatest contribution to Britain's eventual victory – by keeping up the people's morale when all seemed lost. But, once the war against Germany was won, the British public turned their back on Churchill and voted him out of office. Why did this happen?

It is worth pointing out that Churchill's personal popularity during the war tended to vary. In early 1942, less than half the population supported Churchill as Prime Minister. But after 1942, at least seven in every ten supported the government. What seems to have worried the British public was Churchill's qualities as a *peacetime* leader.

The Beveridge Report 1942

In December 1942 Sir William Beveridge presented his report on Britain's social services. He proposed that after the war *all* citizens should be entitled to certain *free* benefits. Most of these benefits, such as unemployment and sickness benefits, existed already but they were not easy to get. Other ideas, such as allowances for children and a National Health Service were new. These benefits would be paid for by contributions from each person's earnings. The benefits only provided a minimum standard of living or care but the Report was tremendously popular.

A Churchill making an election speech from a hotel in High Wycombe, Bucks, in June 1945. Churchill loved the big occasions and he preferred to make a few speeches to big crowds. Attlee, on the other hand, was driven around by his wife and was always in contact with the people. This was something Churchill, with his guards and officials, could not do so easily.

Churchill, though, wasn't keen on the proposals and his lack of interest in them was quickly noticed. The Labour Party, on the other hand, was fully in support of the Beveridge Report. In 1945 voters made it clear which party they trusted to carry out Beveridge's proposals. The voters didn't trust Churchill and his Conservative Party.

Churchill also made some mistakes in the 1945 election campaign. He concentrated on international issues and not domestic ones to do with Britain. Churchill told the voters that communist Russia and its leader, Stalin, were the new threat to Britain. But the people didn't share his worries about communism. They wanted to know about what ideas Churchill had for making Britain a better place to live in.

Churchill and Labour's 'Gestapo'

Churchill had little to say on the things that mattered to the people. They wanted to know how the bombed-out houses would be replaced and what medical treatment they could get under the National Health Service (NHS). Instead of this, Churchill told them that if Labour won the election, they would set up a British version of the Gestapo to keep control.

The Gestapo was Hitler's vicious secret police, responsible for arresting and terrorising opponents. This was a terrible insult to the Labour Party. Labour had not only supported the government in the war against the Nazis but had also been part of the coalition government set up by Churchill.

Labour: 'facing the future'

Churchill had clearly lost touch with the people. Clement Attlee, the Labour leader, on the other hand, was in touch with the public mood. During the election campaign he wisely concentrated on plans for the future of *Britain*. The Labour policy was called 'Let Us Face the Future'. It spelt out how Labour would carry out Beveridge's proposals and **nationalise** key industries like coal, electricity, and the railways. It promised to build four million council homes for those who couldn't afford to buy their own.

Labour won a crushing victory.

Labour won 393 of the 640 seats in the 1945 election and the Conservatives only 213.

Apart from the 1997 election, it was the biggest in its history. Labour's policies matched the public mood with 12 million votes to the Conservatives' ten million. Strangely, one candidate who didn't win was the Liberal, Sir William Beveridge.

The khaki vote

The British people were not prepared to go back to the same Britain which existed before the war. That is what had happened after the First World War. This time things would be different, they decided. It took three weeks for the result of the election in July 1945 to become known. This was because of the 'khaki vote'. These were votes of those men and women serving in the armed forces across the world – especially in the Far East where Japan was still fighting.

They voted in large numbers for Labour. There was considerable ill-feeling between the officers and the lower ranks in the forces, as you can see from source B.

B Frank Mayes, a British communist, remembers the reaction of British sailors to the news of Labour's victory:

> A great cheer went up and one of the officers said, 'Well, that's it. I'm not going back to England.' A sailor said to him, 'Well, we won't bloody miss you.' It was the only time I heard of a seaman speak to an officer like that. We all thought that a fairer, new Britain was going to come about. Of course it didn't, and we were very soon disappointed.

C Vicky, the cartoonist who drew this cartoon in June 1944, was clearly worried about what Britain would be like after the war. The end of the First World War brought only unemployment for its returning soldiers. Would this happen again?

1 What were the main proposals of the Beveridge Report ?
2 Why was Churchill's claim that the Labour Party would need a Gestapo to carry out its policies a stupid thing to say?
3 Why do you think the officer in source B said he wasn't going back to England after hearing the election result?
4 In what ways do sources B and C show similar attitudes to how Britain should be after the war?
5 'Churchill lost the election in 1945 because the people felt he had been a poor leader.' Using the sources and the information in the text, explain whether you agree or disagree with this interpretation.

HOW FAR HAD BRITAIN CHANGED?

The British people were rightly proud of the part they had played in defeating Nazi Germany and then Japan. They felt that it proved that the *British* way of doing things was still best and that Britain was still a great world power. They also felt that the victory now provided an opportunity to rebuild a different and better Britain.

1945: all change?

In some ways, Britain did change. The historian, Arthur Marwick, believes that the war brought about an important change in attitudes. During the war most people came to believe that the government should have a much greater role in running the economy and greater influence over people's lives. This, after all, was how the war had been won. This is exactly what Labour had always believed and explains why the party won the 1945 election so easily. The Labour government's nationalisation policies from 1946–9 reflected this belief.

Britain did change and not just because of new ideas about economic policy. Working-class people, Marwick claims, were no longer prepared to put up with the old pre-war attitudes about class. Many before the war had accepted that rich people, the upper class, were the right people to run the country. But the war gave ordinary people the confidence to take on the job themselves. That's why they voted for Labour.

People came to believe that poverty, slum housing, unemployment, bad diet and poor health could be got rid of. In short, the war led people to expect more from life. They were not going to be fobbed off as they had been after the First World War. The people demanded a 'welfare state' which would provide all these benefits free.

Some historians, like Corelli Barnett, have argued that Britain could not afford to provide these improvements after the war and shouldn't have tried. The war had left Britain owing a huge sum of money. More had to be borrowed from the USA for Britain to pay its bills. Barnett suggests that the money spent on the Welfare State should have been spent on new, up-to-date machinery and equipment for Britain's industries. Only later, when Britain could afford it, should money have been spent on the welfare benefits.

Some **socialist** historians have written that the Labour government of 1945–51 didn't do that much to change British society. The Labour Party's policies between 1945 and 1951, they claim, weren't very socialist at all. Most of what Attlee's Labour government did in these years had already been agreed by the wartime coalition government – a government which included Conservatives. What Labour did was to make **capitalism** work more efficiently and more fairly but they didn't really change the system.

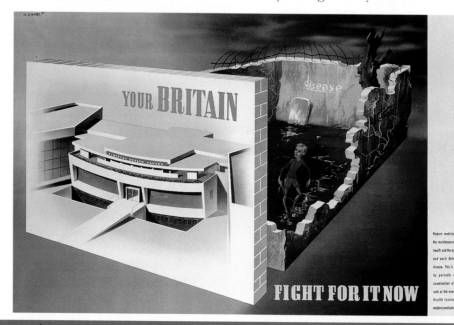

A This poster was issued by the Army Bureau of Current Affairs. The ABCA was an army organis-ation set up in 1941 to encourage education and discussion among the troops. It issued this poster in 1944. It clearly shows its support for the Beveridge Report and implies that disease and slums were still part of Britain at the time. The government ordered the ABCA to withdraw the poster.

B People's memories of the war tend to vary. For some, like the person quoted here, the memories were good ones:

> People were more together. They met in air raid shelters, in the tubes at night, they were in the Home Guard, or they queued for Spam or whatever … Everybody really lost a lot of their shyness about talking to their next door neighbours … and this was the spirit that I think a lot of people hoped would continue after the war.

C Others remember the war for different, sadder reasons. The song referred to here, 'We'll Hang Out Our Washing on the Siegfried Line' was a patriotic wartime song. The Siegfried Line was Germany's defensive line which protected Germany from invasion.

> We were robbed of six years of our lives. The rationing, the black-out … and the deaths of friends and former colleagues in the forces are all different to the idiotic singing we occasionally hear of. 'We'll Hang Out Our Washing on the Siegfried Line' … I never heard anyone singing it.

D The *Daily Mirror* in May 1945 summed up most people's feelings with this cartoon and its caption – 'Here you are! Don't lose it again!' The 'it' was peace. The people were anxious that the peace-makers of 1945 wouldn't make the same mistakes as those in 1919. After the Versailles' Treaty of 1919 the peace of Europe lasted only 20 years.

The end of glory?

The fact that Labour wasn't really very socialist would have been little consolation to Conservatives like Churchill. They had three basic policies for Britain. They wanted to keep Britain as a powerful and independent state, with an important role in world affairs. They wanted to defend the British Empire and they wanted to keep Britain Conservative and Labour out of power.

All these hopes quickly fell apart. Labour won its second biggest election victory ever in 1945. After the war, Britain became very much the junior partner in the relationship between Britain and the United States. Britain gradually lost its role as a major world power. For people like Churchill the worst thing was that by the early 1960s almost all of the British Empire had gone, as each of Britain's colonies became independent.

Churchill lived until 1965 and saw all this happen. A grateful British public recognised its debt to the wartime leader. Churchill was given a State funeral – an honour usually reserved only for kings and queens. 1945 and victory in the war should have been Churchill's most glorious moment. Twenty years later 1945 must have seemed more like the end of glory than its beginning.

1 What was the mood of the British people at the end of the war?
2 How, according to Marwick, did working-class people's attitudes change during the war?
3 What reasons does Marwick suggest for Labour's victory in 1945?
4 Why does Barnett think that the Welfare State was set up at the wrong time?
5 a) In what ways are the memories of the war of the people in sources B and C different?
   b) Since these views are so different, does this mean one of them must be wrong?

Extended writing
'In the long run Britain gained very little from its victory in 1945.' Write a 300-word essay on this question. You should consider this essay from the different points of view discussed in the last few chapters. In what ways, if at all, did the war benefit these groups or help to bring about their ideas?

a) women   c) socialists
b) workers   d) Conservatives

Glossary

Afrika Korps – the German forces which fought in North Africa

air-raid warden – an individual whose job was to help the public during air raids and make sure that air-raid precautions (ARP) were followed

appeasement – a policy of making concessions to avoid conflict; the policy followed by Britain and France towards Germany between 1935 and 1939

Axis – the defeated powers in the war: Germany, Italy and Japan; named after the Rome–Berlin–Tokyo Axis agreement which linked them together

billeting – forcing householders with spare rooms to take in families escaping from the bombing or workers involved in the war effort

Blitzkrieg – a new type of warfare first used by the Germans which achieved the key elements of surprise and speed by using aircraft, tanks and troops transported by trucks

capitalism – an economic system in which the government's role is very limited and businesses are owned privately

censorship – the policy of preventing people from getting information the government wants to keep secret

coalition government – a government made up of two or more political parties working together

communist – someone who believes in a system of government that opposes individual freedom and democracy and favours government control of all major industries

concentration camp – a prison camp where the victims of Nazi racial and political policies were murdered

conscription – forcing men, and sometimes women, to enlist in the armed forces

defeatist – someone who thinks his country will lose the war and lowers morale by saying so

dictator – a ruler who has total control over a country and allows no opposition

fascism – a system of government which opposes individual freedom and democracy and favours extreme nationalism

Fifth Columnist – an enemy spy or supporter of the enemy

Gestapo – The Nazi secret police responsible for arresting opponents inside Germany and the occupied countries

internment – the policy of arresting enemy citizens who live in your country

Lebensraum – the German for 'living space' and Hitler's policy of conquest in the east of Europe

master race – according to Nazi racial theories, the Germans were a superior or master race who were entitled to dominate 'inferior' races like Jews and Slavs

nationalisation – the policy of the government or state taking over one or more privately owned industries

Nazism – a system of government which opposes individual freedom, democracy and favours extreme nationalism and ideas of racial superiority

partisan – a civilian fighter against enemy forces occupying his or her country; also called a resistance fighter. Soldiers, separated from their units, also joined the partisans

provenance – where a source comes from – who wrote it? When? Who was intended to read it? what role did the writer have? Knowing about a source's provenance is important for deciding its value and reliability

Quisling – Vidkun Quisling, a Norwegian, formed a pro-Nazi government in Norway under German control. In 1945 he was executed as a traitor. 'Quisling' has since become a word for traitor or collaborator

raw materials – materials such as coal, iron and oil which are used to manufacture other products

reprisal – the arrest and often execution of hostages in revenge for an attack by resistance groups

SS (*Schutz Staffeln*) – German for protection squads; the SS ran Hitler's concentration camps and committed the worst crimes of the war

Second Front – the invasion of German-occupied France, which finally took place in June 1944 (Russia was the 'first' front)

socialist – someone who believes the government should run the country in the interests of the working people and not the rich

unconditional surrender – when a country surrenders unconditionally it has to accept all the terms imposed by the winners

Vichy France – that part of southern France which the Germans did not occupy. Instead, they allowed a pro-German French government to operate there from the town of Vichy until November 1942